The Industrial Revolution

The Industrial Revolution

by Arnold Toynbee

with a Preface by Arnold J. Toynbee

The Beacon Press Boston

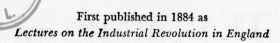

First published in 1884 as
Lectures on the Industrial Revolution in England

First Beacon paperback edition published 1956
Printed in U.S.A.

Sixth printing, May 1964

330.942
Cop. 1

The Industrial Revolution

Preface to the Beacon Paperback Edition

This book is the work of a man who died at the age of thirty. He did not live to write even this one small book with his own hand. It was written for him, after his death, by his friends and pupils, out of the notes they had taken of a course of lectures that he had delivered in 1880-1881 in the University of Oxford and out of his own notes on the subject. This was, for them, a labour of love, and they performed it so skilfully that the book which they have produced bears the authentic stamp of Arnold Toynbee's personality. Because of this personality which shines through the words, this book is one of that small number of books, dealing with matters of fact, that share the privilege of poetry. It will always remain fresh, and therefore will always continue to find readers.

Though Arnold Toynbee's account of the Industrial Revolution does not become 'out of date,' it does, of course, 'date.' One of the features of the book that gives it a lasting interest is that it is a pioneer work. Toynbee was the first economic historian to think of, and to set out to describe, the Industrial Revolution as a single great historical event, in which all the details come together to make an intelligible and significant picture. In doing this, he created the frame within which all subsequent work on the Industrial Revolution has been carried out. The work done during the seventy years since the publication of Toynbee's book has been great in quantity and fine in quality. The evidence has been repeatedly worked over and revised. Masses of additional statistics have been collected and analysed. And, in this sense, Toynbee's work has been superseded long ago. Yet, as a masterly first reconnaissance of a very important field of historical study, this pioneer work by a young man is still as much alive as ever it was.

If it is true that *The Industrial Revolution* is a reflexion of

Arnold Toynbee's personality, the reader may feel curious to learn what Arnold Toynbee was like. Though I am his nephew, I did not have the chance of knowing him myself. I was named for him because I happened to be the first male child bearing his surname to be born into his immediate family after his death in 1883. I did, however, come to know him rather well at second hand, as he appeared in the eyes of people who had known him personally and intimately. His widow, my aunt Charlotte Toynbee, outlived him by nearly fifty years, and several of his colleagues at Balliol College, Oxford, where he had been a tutorial Fellow (that is, a teaching member of the governing body of the college) lived to see the First World War. I was a member of the same college, in my turn, from 1907 to 1915, first as an undergraduate and then as a tutorial Fellow, like my uncle; and the men who had been his contemporaries used often to talk about him and to try to convey to me what it was about him that had made so great a mark at so early a stage in his short life. They all agreed that it was difficult to put their impression of him into words; yet their words did bring out this impression rather clearly, to my mind. The vision that I caught was one of simplicity, sincerity, disinterestedness, and ardour; and these qualities combined to strike an unmistakable note of greatness.

Arnold Toynbee would have made his name simply by virtue of what he achieved. To have produced this book, and to have inspired the foundation of Toynbee Hall as a posthumous memorial to him, were notable achievements for a man who died at thirty. But it was evident to me that his surviving contemporaries revered and loved him for being what he was, even more than for doing what he did.

Death overtook Arnold Toynbee unexpectedly and abruptly. He was in the middle of a debating campaign, in the Lincoln-Douglas manner, with Henry George, the American advocate of a single tax on land, when he was suddenly carried off by a mysterious disease that was diagnosed as 'brain fever' in the medical language of the day. Medicine has made great strides since then, and one may speculate whether, to-day, his life might not have been saved. What might he not have gone on to achieve if he had lived to sixty-six? This tale of years comes into my mind because, at the moment of writing this preface, I myself am in my sixty-seventh year. How famous Arnold Toynbee was at thirty; and how utterly obscure I, for example, among others should have been if I had died at that age. What might not Arnold Toynbee have done if he had lived thirty-six years longer? I have often wondered about this; but I am also sure that, like a truly inspired poet who dies young, Arnold Toynbee was, in one sense, independent of the dole of time. In so far as he achieved greatness, it was through being what he was, and he was his characteristic self already in early manhood. One became aware of this as one listened to his contemporaries talking about him.

ARNOLD J. TOYNBEE

Contents

Contents

I   INTRODUCTORY

(THE subject of these lectures is the Industrial and Agrarian Revolution at the end of the eighteenth and beginning of the nineteenth centuries. The course is divided into three parts. The first deals with Adam Smith and the England of his time. It will describe England on the eve of the Industrial Revolution, and the system of regulation and protection of industry as it existed in 1760. It will give also an outline of Adam Smith's book, its aims and character, and especially his theory of free trade. (The second part will group itself round the work of Malthus, who dealt not so much with the causes of wealth as with the causes of poverty, with the distribution of wealth rather than with its production. It will describe England in the midst of the Industrial Revolution, and will inquire into the problem of pauperism and the subjects connected with it. The third part will be associated with the name of Ricardo, and will deal with England at the time of the Peace. It will discuss the doctrine of rent and wages together with certain theories of economic progress, *and will cover the questions of currency, so much agitated at that period, and the history of the commercial and financial changes which followed the Peace.*)

I have chosen the subject because it was in this period that modern Political Economy took its rise. It has been a weakness of the science, as pursued in England, that it has been too much dissociated from History. Adam Smith and Malthus, indeed, had historical minds; but the form of modern text-books is due to Ricardo, whose mind was entirely unhistorical. Yet there is a double advantage in combining the two studies. In the first place Political Economy is better understood by this means. Abstract propositions are seen in a new light when studied in

1

relation to the facts which were before the writer at the time when he formulated them. So regarded they are at once more vivid and less likely to mislead. Ricardo becomes painfully interesting when we read the history of his time. And, in the second place, History also is better understood when studied in connection with Political Economy; for the latter not only teaches us in reading History to look out for the right kind of facts, but enables us to explain many phenomena like those attending the introduction of enclosures and machinery, or the effects of different systems of currency, which without its assistance would remain unintelligible. The careful deductive reasoning, too, which Political Economy teaches is of great importance to the historian, and the habits of mind acquired from it are even more valuable than the knowledge of principles which it gives, especially to students of facts, who might otherwise be overwhelmed by the mass of their materials.

Of late years, however, there has been a steady sustained attack upon the abstract Deductive Method of Political Economy pursued by Ricardo and Mill, and an attempt to set up historical investigation in its place as the only true method of economic inquiry. This attack rests on a misconception of the function of the Deductive Method. The best exposition of the place of Abstract Political Economy is to be found in Bagehot's *Economic Studies*. Bagehot points out that this abstract science holds good only upon certain assumptions, but though the assumptions are often not entirely correct, the results may yet be approximately true. Thus the economists, firstly, regard only one part of man's nature, and treat him simply as a money-making animal; secondly, they disregard the influence of custom, and only take account of competition. Certain laws are laid down under these assumptions; as, for instance, that the rate of wages always tends to an equality, the permanent difference obtaining in various employments being only sufficient to balance the favourable or unfavourable circumstances attending each of them—a law which is only true after a certain stage of civilisation and in so far as the acquisition of wealth is the sole object of men. Such hypothetical laws, though leading only to rough conclusions, are yet useful in giving us a point of view from which to observe and indicate the existence of strong overmastering tendencies. Advocates of the Historical Method, like Mr. Cliffe Leslie, therefore, go too far when they condemn the Deductive Method as radically false. There is no real opposition between the two. The apparent opposition is due to a wrong use of deduction; to a neglect on the part of those employing it to examine closely their assumptions and to bring their conclusions to the test of fact; to arguments based on premises which are not only not verified but absolutely untrue (as in the wage-fund theory); and generally to the failure to combine induction with deduction. But this misuse of the method does not imply any radical faultiness in it. The right method in any particular case must be largely determined by the nature of the problem. Neither is it fair to make abstract Political Economy responsible for the confusion in many minds between its laws and the precepts which are based on them. It is a pure science, and its end is knowledge. But the Political Economy of the press and the platform is a practical science, that is, a body of rules and maxims to guide conduct. Journalists and members of Parliament confound the laws of the pure science with the maxims of the practical science. It was thus that Mr. Gladstone in the Land Act controversy of 1881 was constantly accused of violating the laws of Political Economy. It was impossible for Mr. Gladstone to do any such thing. The laws of Political Economy can no more be violated than those of physical science. What the journalists meant was that he had departed from a great economic precept—that which recommends freedom of contract.

The Historical Method pursues a different line of investigation. It examines the actual causes of economic development and considers the influence of institutions, such as the mediæval guilds, our present land-laws, or the political constitution of any given country, in determining the distribution of wealth. Without the aid of the Historical Method it would be impossible, for instance, to understand why one-half of the land in the United Kingdom is owned by 2512 persons.[2]

And not only does it investigate the stages of economic development in a given country, but it compares them with those which have obtained in other countries and times, and seeks by such comparison to discover laws of universal application. Take, as an instance of the discoveries of this Comparative Political Economy, the tendency which Sir H. Maine and M. de Laveleye have pointed out to pass from collective to individual ownership of land. This is a law which is true of nearly all civilised countries. We must be careful, however, not to generalise too hastily in these matters. A clever pamphlet lately published in Dublin appeals to another generalisation of Sir H. Maine—'Maine's Law,' as it is denominated—in condemnation of recent legislation. 'Sir H. Maine,' says the writer, 'in his *Ancient Law* has remarked that the movement of all progressive societies has hitherto been a movement from status to contract. The demand of this agitation is that Ireland should be legislatively declared a retrograde society, and that the social movement should be from contract back again to status.' [3] 'Is it expedient,' asks another, 'to reform our laws so as to assimilate them to those in use among nations of an inferior social development?' [4] A deeper study of existing civilisation in England, and of other civilisations, past and present, would have shown that the step was not a retrograde one—that whilst the sphere of contract has been widening, it has been also narrowing, and that such a condition of things as we see in Ireland has never existed anywhere else without deep social misery, outrage, and disturbance. Custom or law or public opinion, or all three, have intervened in the past, and will intervene in the future. It is true that there is a movement from status to contract; yet if we look closely, we find that the State has over and over again had to interfere to restrict the power of individuals in which this movement results. The real course of development has been first from status to contract, then from contract to a new kind of status determined by the law—or, in other words, from unregulated to regulated contract.

The Historical Method is also of value because it makes us see where economic laws and precepts are relative.[5] The old economists were wont to speak as if these laws and precepts were universal. Free trade, for instance, is a sound policy, no doubt, for England, and for all nations at a certain stage of development; but it is open to any one to say that free trade is only good under certain conditions. No English economist, it is true, has dared to say this. Mr. Jevons, to take an example, would admit restrictions only for considerations of the most paramount importance.[6] But it is an unjustifiable prejudgment of the question to lay down that this policy must be wise at all times and places. I do not mean to assert, however, that there are not some laws which are universally true, such as the law of diminishing returns.

This discussion about method may seem barren, but it is not really so. Take such a question as the functions of the State. Mr. Senior spent much time in attempting to discover an universal formula which should define their proper limit all the world over. Such an attempt must be abandoned. The proper limits of Government interference are relative to the nature of each particular state and the stage of its civilisation. It is a matter of great importance at the present day for us to discover what these limits are in our own case, for administration bids fair to claim a large share of our attention in the future. It would be well if, in studying the past,[7] we could aways bear in mind the problems of the present, and go to that past to seek large views of what is of lasting importance to the human race. It is an old complaint that histories leave out of sight those vital questions which are connected with the condition of the people. The French Revolution has indeed profoundly modified our views of history, but much still remains to be done in that direction. If I could persuade some of those present to study Economic History, to follow out the impulse originally given by Malthus to the study of the history of the mass of the people, I should be indeed glad. Party historians go to the past for party purposes; they seek to read into the past the controversies of the present. You must pursue facts for their own sake, but penetrated with a vivid sense of the problems of your own time. This is not a principle of perversion, but a principle of selection.

You must have some principle of selection, and you could not have a better one than to pay special attention to the history of the social problems which are agitating the world now, for you may be sure that they are problems not of temporary but of lasting importance.

Population

PREVIOUSLY to 1760 the old industrial system obtained in England; none of the great mechanical inventions had been introduced; the agrarian changes were still in the future. It is this industrial England which we have to contrast with the industrial England of to-day. For determining the population of the time we have no accurate materials. There are no official returns before 1801. A census had been proposed in 1753, but rejected as 'subversive of the last remains of English liberty.' [1] In this absence of trustworthy data all sorts of wild estimates were formed. During the American War a great controversy raged on this subject. Dr. Price, an advocate of the Sinking Fund, maintained that population had in the interval between 1690 and 1777 declined from 6,596,075 to 4,763,670.[2] On the other hand, Mr. Howlett, Vicar of Dunmow, in Essex, estimated the population in 1780 at 8,691,000,[3] and Arthur Young, in 1770, at 8,500,000 on the lowest estimate.[4] These, however, are the extremes in either direction. The computations now most generally accepted are those made by Mr. Finlaison (Actuary to the National Debt Office), and published in the Preface to the Census Returns of 1831. These are based on an examination of the registers of baptisms and burials of the eighteenth century. But the data are deficient in three respects: because the number of people existing at the date when the computation begins is a matter of conjecture; because in some parishes there were no registers; and because the registration, being voluntary, was incomplete.[5] Mr. Finlaison, however, is stated to have subjected his materials to 'every test suggested by the present comparatively advanced state of physical and statistical science.' [6]

Now according to Mr. Finlaison, the population of England and Wales was, in 1700, 5,134,516, in 1750, 6,039,684, an increase of not quite a million, or between 17 and 18 per cent. in the first half of the century.[7] In 1801 the population of England and Wales was 9,187,176, showing an increase of three millions, or more than 52 per cent. in the second half.[8] The difference in the rate of increase is significant of the great contrast presented by the two periods. In the former, England, though rapidly increasing in wealth owing to her extended commercial relations, yet retained her old industrial organisation; the latter is the age of transition to the modern industrial system, and to improved methods of agriculture.

The next point to consider is the distribution of population. A great difference will be found here between the state of things at the beginning of the eighteenth century, or in Adam Smith's time, and that prevailing now. Every one remembers Macaulay's famous description in the beginning of his history of the desolate condition of the northern counties. His picture is borne out by Defoe, who, in his *Tour through the Whole Island* (1725), remarks: 'The country south of Trent is by far the largest, as well as the richest and most populous,' though the great cities were rivalled by those of the north.[9] If we consider as the counties north of Trent Northumberland, Durham, Yorkshire, Cumberland, Westmoreland, Lancashire, Cheshire, Derbyshire, Nottinghamshire, and Staffordshire (about one-third of the total area of England), we shall find on examination that in 1700 they contained about one-fourth of the population,[10] and in 1750 less than one-third,[11] while in 1881, they contained more than two-fifths;[12] or, taking only the six northern counties, we find that in 1700 their population was under one-fifth of that of all England, in 1750 it was about one-fifth, in 1881 it was all but one-third.[13]

In 1700 the most thickly peopled counties (excluding the metropolitan counties of Middlesex and Surrey) were Gloucestershire, Somerset, and Wilts, the manufacturing districts of the west; Worcestershire and Northamptonshire, the seats of the Midland manufactures; and the agriculture counties of Herts and Bucks—all of them being south of the Trent. Between 1700 and 1750 the greatest increase of population took place in the following counties:

Lancashire increased from		166,200	to	297,400,	or	78	per cent.
Warwickshire	"	96,000	"	140,000,	"	45	"
The West Riding of Yorkshire	"	} 236,700	"	361,500,	"	52	"
Durham	"	95,000	"	135,000,	"	41	"
Staffordshire	"	117,200	"	160,000,	"	36	"
Gloucestershire	"	155,200	"	207,800,	"	34	"

Cornwall, Kent, Berks, Herts, Worcestershire, Salop, Cheshire, Northumberland, Cumberland, and Westmoreland each increased upwards of 20 per cent.[14]

The change in the distribution of population between the beginning of the eighteenth century and Adam Smith's time, and again between his time and our own, may be further illustrated by the following table. The twelve most densely populated counties and their density to the square mile were:

1700		1750		1881	
Middlesex	2221	Middlesex	2283	Middlesex	10,387
Surrey	207	Surrey	276	Surrey	1,919
Gloucester	123	Warwick	159	Lancashire	1,813
Northampton .	121	Gloucester	157	Durham	891
Somerset	119	Lancashire	156	Stafford	862
Worcester	119	Worcester	148	Warwick	825
Herts	115	Herts	141	West Riding ..	815
Wilts	113	Stafford	140	Kent	600
Bucks	110	Durham	138	Cheshire	582
Rutland	110	Somerset	137	Worcester	515
Warwick	109	West Riding ..	135	Nottingham ..	475
Oxford	107	Berks	131	Gloucester	455

The most suggestive fact in the period between 1700 and 1750 is the great increase in the Lancashire and the West Riding, the seats of the cotton and coarse woollen manufactures. Staffordshire and Warwickshire, with their potteries and hardware, had also largely grown. So had the two northern counties of Durham and Northumberland, with their coalfields. The West of England woollen districts of Somerset, and Wilts, on the other hand, though they had grown also, showed nothing like so great an increase. The population of the eastern counties Norfolk, Suffolk, and Essex, had increased very little; though Norwich was still a large manufacturing town, and there were many smaller towns engaged in the woollen trade scattered throughout Norfolk and Suffolk. Among the few agricultural counties which showed a decided increase during this period was Kent, the best farmed county in England at that time.

If we turn to the principal towns we shall find in many of them an extraordinary growth between the end of the seventeenth century and the time of Adam Smith. While the population of Norwich had only increased, according to the best authority, by about one-third, and that of Worcester by one-half, the population of Sheffield had increased seven-fold, that of Liverpool ten-fold, of Manchester five-fold, of Birmingham seven-fold, of Bristol more than three-fold. The latter was still the second city in the kingdom. Newcastle (including Gateshead and North and South Shields) numbered 40,000 people.

The following are the estimates of population for 1685, 1760, and 1881 in twelve great provincial towns:—

	1685	c. 1760	1881[g]
Liverpool	4,000[a]	40,000[c] 30-35,000[d] 34,000[e]	552,425
Manchester	6,000[a]	30,000[c] 40-45,000[d]	393,676
Birmingham	4,000[a]	28,000[b] 30,000[d]	400,757
Leeds	7,000[a]	——	309,126
Sheffield	4,000[a]	30,000[c] 20,000[d]	284,410
Bristol	29,000[a]	100,000[d]	206,503
Nottingham	8,000[a]	17,000[f]	111,631
Norwich	28,000[a]	40,000[c] 60,000[d]	87,843
Hull	——	20,000[c] 24,000[d]	161,519
York	10,000[a]	——	59,596
Exeter	10,000[a]	——	47,098
Worcester	8,000[a]	11-12,000[c]	40,421

[a] Macaulay's *History of England*, c. 3.   [b] Defoe's *Tour* (1725).
[c] Arthur Young (1769).   [d] Macpherson's *Annals of Commerce* (1760).
[e] Levi's *History of British Commerce*.   [f] Eden's *State of the Poor* (1797).
[g] The returns for 1881 are those of the parliamentary district.

Another point to be considered is the relation of rural to urban population. According to Gregory King, writing in 1696,

London contained 530,000 inhabitants, other cities and market-towns, 870,000, while villages and hamlets numbered 4,100,000.[15] Arthur Young, seventy years later, calculated that London contained one-sixth of the whole population,[16] and remarked that, 'in flourishing countries,' as England, 'the half of a nation is found in towns.' [17] Both estimates are very unreliable, apart from the fact that both, and especially that of Arthur Young, overestimate the total number of the population, but the contrast between them justly indicates the tendency of towns even then to grow out of proportion to the rural districts. That disproportion has, of course, become even more marked since Arthur Young's day. In 1881 the total urban population was 17,285,026, or 66.6 per cent., while the rural was 8,683,026, or 33.3 per cent.[18]

The only estimates of occupations with which I am acquainted are again those of Gregory King in 1696, and Arthur Young in 1769. They are too vague, and too inconsistent with one another, to be relied on, but I give them for what they are worth. According to the former, freeholders and their families numbered 940,000, farmers and their families, 750,000, labouring people and out servants, 1,275,000, cottagers and paupers, 1,300,000; making a total agricultural population of 4,265,000, against only 240,000 artisans and handicraftsmen.[19] Arthur Young estimates the number of different classes as follows:—

Farmers (whether freeholders or leaseholders), their servants and labourers	2,800,000
Manufacturers of all kinds	3,000,000
Landlords and their dependants, fishermen and miners	800,000
Persons engaged in commerce	700,000
Non-industrious poor	500,000
Clergy and lawyers	200,000
Civil servants, army and navy	500,000
Total	8,500,000[20]

But the number set down to manufactures here is probably as much too high, in proportion to the total population, as the total itself is in excess of the fact.

Agriculture

IN describing the agriculture of the time the first point of importance is the proportion of cultivated land to waste. Gregory King, who rather overestimated the total acreage of England and Wales, put the arable land at 11,000,000 acres, pasture and meadow at 10,000,000, houses, gardens, orchards, etc., at 1,000,000, being a total of 22,000,000 acres of cultivated land, or nearly three-fifths of the whole country.[1] A land-agent in 1727 believed one-half of the country to be waste.[2] Arthur Young, writing fifty years later, puts the cultivated area at a much higher figure. Estimating the total acreage of England alone at 34,000,000 acres, he considered that 32,000,000 of these were in arable and pasture, in equal proportions.[3]

One or other of the two first-mentioned estimates is certainly nearer the truth than the last. The exact proportion is, however, impossible to determine.

There is no respect in which the agricultural England of to-day differs more from that of the period which we are considering, than in the greatly reduced amount of common land. The enclosure of commons had been going on for centuries before 1760, but with nothing like the rapidity with which it has been going on since. It is known that 334,974 acres were enclosed between 1710 and 1760, while nearly 7,000,000 were enclosed between 1760 and 1843.[4] At the beginning of the latter period a large proportion of this land, since enclosed, was under the primitive tillage of the common-fields. Throughout considerable districts the agrarian system of the middle ages still existed in full force. Some parishes had no common or waste lands belonging to them, but where common lands were cultivated, one and the same plan was generally pursued. The arable land of each village was divided into three great stripes subdivided by 'baulks' three yards wide.[5] Every farmer would own at least one piece of land in each field, and all were bound to follow the customary tillage. One strip was left fallow every year; on the other two were grown wheat and barley; sometimes oats, pease, or tares were substituted for the latter. The meadows were also held in common. Up to hay harvest, indeed, every man had his own plot, but, while in the arable land the plots rarely changed hands, in the meadows the different shares were apportioned by lot every year. After hay-harvest the fences in the meadow land were thrown down, and all householders had common rights of grazing on it. Similarly the stubbles were grazed, but here the right was rarely open to all. Every farmer had the right of pasture on the waste.

Though these common fields contained the best soil in the kingdom, they exhibited the most wretched cultivation. 'Never,' says Arthur Young, 'were more miserable crops seen than all the spring ones in the common fields; absolutely beneath contempt.'[6] The causes of this deficient tillage were three in number: (1) The same course of crops was necessary. No proper rotation was feasible; the only possible alternation being to vary the proportions of different white-straw crops. There were no turnips or artificial grasses, and consequently no sheep-farming on a large scale. Such sheep as there were were miserably small; the whole carcase weighed only 28 lbs., and the fleeces $3\frac{1}{2}$ lbs. each, as against 9 lbs. on sheep in enclosed fields.[7] (2) Much time was lost by labourers and cattle 'in travelling to many dispersed pieces of land from one end of a parish to another.'[8] (3) Perpetual quarrels arose about rights of pasture in the meadows and stubbles, and respecting boundaries; in some fields there were no 'baulks' to divide the plots, and men would plough by night to steal a furrow from their neighbours.[9]

For these reasons the connections between the practice of enclosing and improved agriculture was very close. The early enclosures, made under the Statutes of Merton (1235), and Westminster (1285), were taken by the lords of the manor from the waste. But in these cases the lord had first to prove that sufficient pasturage had been left for the commoners; and if rights

of common existed independent of the possession of land, no
enclosure was permitted. These early enclosures went on steadily, but the enclosures which first attract notice towards the end
of the fifteenth century were of a different kind. They were often
made on cultivated land, and, if Nasse is correct, they took the
form not only of permanent conversions from arable into pasture, but of temporary conversions of arable into pasture, followed by reconversion from pasture into arable. The result was
a great increase of produce. The lord having separated his plots
from those of his neighbours, and having consolidated them,
could pursue any system of tillage which seemed good to him.
The alternate and convertible husbandry, mentioned above, was
introduced; the manure of the cattle enriched the arable land,
and 'the grass crops on the land ploughed up and manured were
much stronger and of a better quality than those on the constant
pasture.'[10] Under the old system the manure was spread on the
ground pasture, while in the enclosures it was used for the bene-
fit of land broken up for tillage. The great enclosures of the
sixteenth century took place in Suffolk, Essex, Kent, and Northamptonshire, which were in consequence the most wealthy counties.[11] They were frequent also in Oxford, Berks, Warwickshire,
Bedfordshire, Bucks, and Leicestershire, and with similar results.
In Arthur Young's time Norfolk, Suffolk, Essex, and Kent were
the best cultivated parts of England.

Taking a general view of the state of agriculture in 1760, we
find that improvements were confined to a few parts of the
country. The first enclosure Bill (1710) was to legalise the enclosure of a parish in Hampshire. I have looked through twelve
of these Bills of the reign of George I., and I find that they applied to parishes in Derbyshire, Lancashire, Yorkshire, Staffordshire, Somersetshire, Gloucestershire, Wilts, Warwickshire, and
Norfolk.[12] But though enclosures were thus widely distributed,
certain counties continued to bear a much higher reputation
than others, and in some improvements were confined to one or
two parishes, and not spread over a wide district. The best cultivated counties were those which had long been enclosed. Kent,
which was spoken of by William Stafford in 1581 as a county

where much of the land was enclosed, is described by Arthur
Young as having 'long been reckoned the best cultivated in England.' . . . 'It must astonish strangers,' he says, 'to East Kent and
Thanet, to find such numbers of *common* farmers that have more
drilled crops than broadcast ones, and to see them so familiar
with drill-ploughs and horse-hoes. The drill culture carried on
in so complete a manner is the great peculiarity of this country.
. . . Hops are extremely well cultivated.'[13] In another passage
he says that Kent and Hertfordshire 'have the reputation of
a very accurate cultivation.'[14] The Marquis of Rockingham
brought a Hertfordshire farmer to teach his tenants in the West
Riding to hoe turnips.[15] The husbandry both of that district
and of the East Riding was very backward. The courses of crops
and the general management of the arable land were very faulty;
very few of the farmers hoed turnips, and those who did executed
the work in so slovenly a way that neither the crop nor the land
was the least the better for it; beans were never hoed at all.[16]
The husbandry of Northumberland, on the other hand, was
much superior to that of Durham and Yorkshire. Turnips were
hoed, manure was better managed, and potatoes were cultivated
on a large scale.[17] Essex, held up by Tusser in the reign of Elizabeth as an example of the advantages of enclosures,[18] and described by Young in 1807 as having 'for ages been an enclosed
country,' is mentioned as early as 1694 as a county where 'some
have their fallow after turnips, which feed their sheep in winter,'[19]—the first mention of turnips as a field crop.

But the greatest progress in the first half of the eighteenth century seems to have taken place in Norfolk. Every one has heard
of Townshend growing turnips at Raynham, after his quarrel
with Walpole; and Young, writing in 1812, after speaking of the
period 1700-1760 as one of stagnation, owing to low prices ('it
is absolutely vain to expect improvements in agriculture unless
prices are more disposed to rise than to remain long without
variations that give encouragement to the farmer'), admits that
the improvements made in Norfolk during that time were an exception. In his *Eastern Tour* (1770), he had spoken of the husbandry 'which has rendered the name of this county so famous

in the farming world';[20] and given seven reasons for the improvements. These were: (1) Enclosing without assistance of Parliament. Parliamentary enclosure 'through the knavery of commissioners and attorneys,' was very expensive. 'Undoubtedly many of the finest loams on the richest marls would at this day have been sheep-walks had there been any right of commonage on them';[21] (2) Marling, for there was plenty of marl under the sand everywhere; (3) An excellent rotation of crops—the famous Norfolk four years' course of turnips, barley, clover (or clover and rye-grass), and wheat; (4) The culture of turnips well hand-hoed; (5) The culture of clover and rye-grass; (6) The granting of long leases;[22] (7) The division of the county chiefly into large farms. 'Great farms,' he says, 'have been the soul of the Norfolk culture,[23] though in the eastern part of the county there were little occupiers of £100 a year.[24]

Throughout the whole of the South of England, however, there had been a certain amount of progress. Hoeing turnips, according to Young, was common in many parts of the south of the kingdom,[25] although the extensive use of turnips—*i.e.* all their uses for fattening cattle as well as feeding lean sheep—'is known but little of, except in Norfolk, Suffolk, and Essex.'[26] Clover husbandry, on the other hand, was 'universal from the North of England to the further end of Glamorganshire.' Clover, the 'great clover,' had been introduced into England by Sir Richard Weston about 1645, as had probably been turnips also. Potatoes at the beginning of the century were only garden crops. Hemp and flax were frequently grown, as were also hops, which had been introduced in the beginning of the sixteenth century.

If we turn from the cultivation of the soil to the management and breeding of live stock, we shall find that no great progress had been made in this branch during the years 1700-1760. Davenant in 1700 estimated the net carcase of black cattle at 370 lb., and of a sheep at 28 lb. A century later Eden calculated that 'bullocks now killed in London weigh, at an average, 800 lb., sheep 80 lb., and lambs about 50 lb. each';[27] and Young in 1786 put the weight of bullocks and sheep at 840 lb. and 100 lb. respectively. But this improvement seems to have come about after 1760. It was not until 1760-85 that Bakewell perfected the new breed of sheep—the Leicesters—and improved the breed of long-horned cattle, and that the brothers Culley obtained the short-horn, or Durham cattle, from the breed in the valley of the Tees.[28] Some improvements in the breed of sheep, however, had already been made. 'The wool of Warwickshire, Northamptonshire, Lincolnshire, and Rutland, with some parts of Huntingdon, Bedford, Buckinghamshire, Cambridgeshire, and Norfolk has been accounted the longest and finest combing wool. But of late years' (this was written in 1739) 'there have been improvements made in the breed of sheep by changing or rams and sowing of turnips and grass seeds, and now there is some large fine combing wool to be found in most counties in England, which is fine, long, and soft, fit to make all sorts of fine stuff and hose of.'[29] Still improvements in feeding sheep were by no means universally adopted for half a century later.[30] Agricultural implements, too, were still very primitive, wooden ploughs being commonly in use,[31] while the small, narrow-wheeled waggon of the North held 40 or 50 bushels with difficulty.

Arthur Young constantly attributes much of the bad agriculture to the low rentals prevalent. 'Of so little encouragement to them,' he writes of the farmers of Cleveland, 'is the lowness of their rents, that many large tracts of land that yielded good crops of corn within thirty years are now overrun with whins, brakes, and other trumpery. . . . If I be demanded how such ill courses are to be stopped, I answer, Raise their rents. First with moderation, and if that does not bring forth industry, double them.'[32] At the same time Young strongly advocated long leases. But it must be remembered that besides tenant-farmers there were still a large number of freeholders and still more copyholders either for life or by inheritance.

On the whole, though the evidence on some points is somewhat contradictory, the progress of agriculture between 1700 and 1760 may be said to have been slow. Writing in 1770 Arthur Young ascribes to the last ten years 'more experiments, more discoveries, and more general good sense displayed in the walk of agriculture than in an hundred preceding ones.' Though drill-husbandry was practised by Jethro Tull, 'a gentleman of Berkshire,' as early as 1701, and his book was published in 1731, 'he seems to have had few followers in England for more than thirty years,'[33] and Young in 1770 speaks of 'the new husbandry' as having sunk with Tull, and 'not again put in motion till within a few years.'[34] On the other hand, we have as early as 1687 Petty's notice of 'the draining of fens, watering of dry grounds, and improving of forests and commons.' Macpherson in the year 1729 speaks of the great sums lately expended in the enclosing and improving of lands;[35] and Laurence in 1727 asserts that 'it is an undoubted truth that the Art of Husbandry is of late years greatly improved, and accordingly many estates have already admitted their utmost improvement, but,' he adds, 'much the greater number still remains of such as are so far from being brought to that perfection that they have felt few or none of the effects of modern arts and experiments.'[36]

Still, in spite of the ignorance and stupidity of the farmers and their use of wretched implements, the average produce of wheat was large. In 1770 it was twenty-five bushels to the acre, when in France it was only eighteen.[37] At the beginning of the century some of our colonies imported wheat from the mother country. The average export of grain from 1697 to 1765 was nearly 500,000 quarters, while the imports came to a very small figure. The exports were sent to Russia, Holland, and America.

Manufactures and Trade

AMONG the manufactures of the time the woollen business was by far the most important. 'All our measures,' wrote Bishop Berkeley in 1737, 'should tend towards the immediate encouragement of our woollen manufactures, which must be looked upon as the basis of our wealth.' In 1701 our woollen exports were worth £2,000,000, or 'above a fourth part of the whole export trade.'[1] In 1770 they were worth £4,000,000, or between a third and a fourth of the whole.[2] The territorial distribution of the manufacture was much the same as now. This industry had probably existed in England from an early date. It is mentioned in a law of 1224.[3] In 1331 John Kennedy brought the art of weaving woollen cloth from Flanders into England, and received the protection of the king, who at the same time invited over fullers and dyers. There is extant a petition of the worsted-weavers and merchants of Norwich to Edward III. in 1348. The coarse cloths of Kendal and the fine cloths of Somerset, Dorset, Bristol, and Gloucester are mentioned in the statutes of the same century. In 1391 we hear of Guildford cloths, and in 1467 of the woollen manufacture in Devonshire—at Lifton, Tavistock, and Rowburgh. In 1402 the manufacture was settled to a great extent in and near London, but it gradually shifted, owing to the high price of labour and provisions, to Surrey, Kent, Essex, Berkshire, and Oxfordshire, and afterwards still further, into the counties of Dorset, Wilts, Somerset, Gloucester, and Worcester, and even as far as Yorkshire.

There were three chief districts in which the woollen trade was carried on about 1760. One of these owed its manufacture to the wars in the Netherlands. In consequence of Alva's persecutions (1567-8) many Flemings settled in Norwich (which had been desolate since Ket's rebellion in 1549), Colchester, Sand-

wich, Canterbury, Maidstone, and Southampton. The two former towns seem to have benefited most from the skill of these
settlers so far as the woollen manufacture was concerned. It was
at this time, according to Macpherson, that Norwich 'learned the
making of those fine and slight stuffs which have ever since gone
by its name,' such as crapes, bombazines, and camblets; while
the baize-makers settled at Colchester and its neighbourhood.
The stuffs thus introduced into England were known as the
'new drapery,' and included baize, serges, and other slight woollen goods as distinguished from the 'old drapery,' a term applied
to broad cloth, kersies, etc.

The chief seats of the West of England manufacture were
Bradford in Wilts, the centre of the manufacture of super-fine
cloth; Devizes, famous for its serges; Warminster and Frome,
with their fine cloth; Trowbridge; Stroud, the centre of the dyed-
cloth manufactures; and Taunton, which in Defoe's time possessed 1100 looms.[4] The district reached from Cirencester in the
north to Sherborne in the south, and from Witney in the east
to Bristol in the west, being about fifty miles in length where
longest, and twenty in breadth where narrowest—'a rich enclosed country,' as Defoe says, 'full of rivers and towns, and
infinitely populous, insomuch that some of the market towns are
equal to cities in bigness, and superior to many of them in numbers of people.' It was a 'prodigy of a trade,' and the 'fine Spanish medley cloths' which this district produced were worn by
'all the persons of fashion in England.'[5] It was no doubt the
presence of streams and the Cotswold wool which formed the
attractions of the district. A branch of the industry extended
into Devon, where the merchants of Exeter bought in a rough
state the serges made in the country round, to dye and finish
them for home consumption or export.

The third chief seat of the manufacture was the West Riding
of Yorkshire, where the worsted trade centred round Halifax,
which, according to Camden, began to manufacture about 1537;
and where Leeds and its neighbourhood manufactured a coarse
cloth of English wool. In 1574 the manufacturers of the West

Riding made 56,000 pieces of broad cloth and 72,000 of narrow. It will be seen from this short survey that, however greatly the production of these different districts may have changed in proportion since 1760, the several branches of the trade are even now distributed very much as they were then, the West Riding being the headquarters of the worsted and coarse cloth trade, while Norwich still keeps the crape industry, and the West manufactures fine cloth.

The increased demand for English wool consequent upon the extension of this industry led to large enclosures of land, especially in Northamptonshire, Rutlandshire, Leicestershire, and Warwickshire, which counties supplied most of the combing wools used for worsted stuffs and stockings; but parts of Huntingdon, Bedford, Bucks, Cambridgeshire, Romney Marsh, and Norfolk competed with them, and by 1739 most counties produced the fine combing wool. Defoe mentions the sale of wool from Lincolnshire, 'where the longest staple is found, the sheep of those parts being of the largest breed';[6] and in Arthur Young's time Lincolnshire and Leicestershire wools were still used at Norwich.[7] The Cotswold and Isle of Wight sheep yielded clothing or short wools, 'but they were inferior to the best Spanish wools,' and could not 'enter into the composition without spoiling and degrading in some degree the fabric of the cloth.'[8] Consequently in the West of England, occupied as it was with the production of the finest cloths, Spanish wool was largely used, though shortly before Young's time it was discovered that 'Norfolk sheep yielded a wool about their necks equal to the best from Spain.'[9]

Next in importance was the iron trade, which was largely carried on, though by this time a decaying industry, in the Weald of Sussex, where in 1740 there were ten furnaces, producing annually 1400 tons. The trade had reached its chief extent in the seventeenth century, but in 1724 was still the principal manufacturing interest of the county. The balustrades which surround St. Paul's were cast at Lamberhurst, and their weight, including the seven gates, is above 200 tons. They cost £11,000. Gloucestershire, Shropshire, and Yorkshire had each six furnaces. In the latter county, which boasted an annual produce of 1400[10] tons, the most famous works were at Rotherham. There were also great ironworks at Newcastle.[11]

In 1755 an ironmaster named Anthony Bacon had got a lease for ninety-nine years of a district eight miles in length, by five in breadth, at Merthyr-Tydvil, upon which he erected iron and coal works.[12] In 1709 the Coalbrookdale works in Shropshire were founded, and in 1760 Carron iron was first manufactured in Scotland.[13] Altogether, there were about 1737 fifty-nine furnaces in eighteen different counties, producing 17,350 tons annually. It has been computed that we imported 20,000 tons.[14] In 1881 we exported 3,820,315 tons of iron and steel, valued at £27,590,-908, and imported to the value of £3,705,332.

The cotton trade was still so insignificant as to be mentioned only once, and that incidentally by Adam Smith. It was confined to Lancashire, where its headquarters were Manchester and Bolton. In 1760 not more than 40,000 persons were engaged in it, and the annual value of the manufactures was estimated at £600,000. The exports, however, were steadily growing; in 1701 they amounted to £23,253, in 1751 to £45,986, in 1764 to £200,-354. Burke about this time spoke of 'that infinite variety of admirable manufactures that grow and extend every year among the spirited, inventive, and enterprising traders of Manchester.' But even in 1764 our exports of cotton were still only one-twentieth of the value of the wool exports.

The hardware trade then as now was located chiefly in Sheffield and Birmingham, the latter town employing over 50,000 people in that industry.[15] The business, however, was not so much concentrated as now, and there were small workshops scattered about the kingdom. 'Polished steel,' for instance, was manufactured at Woodstock, locks in South Staffordshire, pins at Warrington, Bristol, and Gloucester, where they were 'the staple of the city.'[16]

The hosiery trade, too, was as yet only in process of concentration. By 1800 the manufacture of silk hosiery had centred in Derby, that of woollen hosiery in Leicester, though Nottingham had not yet absorbed the cotton hosiery. But at the beginning of the century there were still many looms round London, and in other parts of the South of England. In 1750 London had 1000 frames, Surrey 350, Nottingham 1500, Leicester 1000, Derby 200, other places in the Midlands, 7300; other English and Scotch towns, 1850; Ireland, 800; Total, 14,000.[17] Most of the silk was woven in Spitalfields, but first spun in the North at Stockport, Knutsford, Congleton, and Derby.[18] In 1770 there was a silk-mill at Sheffield on the model of Derby, and a manufactory of waste silk at Kendal.[19] Coventry had already, in Defoe's time, attracted the ribbon business.[20] In 1721 the silk manufacture was said to be worth £700,000 a year more than at the Revolution.[21]

Linen was an ancient manufacture in England, and had been introduced into Dundee at the beginning of the seventeenth century. In 1746 the British Linen Company was incorporated to supply Africa and the American plantations with linen made at home,[22] and Adam Smith considered it a growing manufacture. It was, of course, the chief manufacture of Ireland, where it had been further developed by French Protestants, who settled there at the end of the seventeenth century.

The mechanical arts were still in a very backward state. In spite of the fact that the woollen trade was the staple industry of the country, the division of labour in it was in Adam Smith's time 'nearly the same as it was a century before, and the machinery employed not very different.' According to the same author there had been only three inventions of importance since Edward iv.'s reign: the exchange of the rock and spindle for the spinning-wheel; the use of machines for facilitating the proper arrangement of the warp and woof before being put into the loom; and the employment of fulling mills for thickening cloth instead of treading it in water. In this enumeration, however, he forgot to mention the fly-shuttle, invented in 1738 by Kay, a native of Bury, in Lancashire, the first of the great inventions which revolutionised the woollen industry. Its utility consisted in its enabling a weaver to do his work in half the time, and making it possible for one man instead of two to weave the widest cloth.[23]

'The machines used in the cotton manufacture,' says Baines,

'were, up to the year 1760, nearly as simple as those of India
though the loom was more strongly and perfectly constructed
and cards for combing the cotton had been adapted from the
woollen manufacture. None but the strong cottons, such as
fustians and dimities, were as yet made in England, and for these
the demand must always have been limited.'[24] In 1738 John
Wyatt invented spinning by rollers, but the discovery never
proved profitable. In 1760 the manufacturers of Lancashire be
gan to use the fly-shuttle. Calico printing was already largely
developed.[25]

The reason why division of labour was carried out to so small
an extent, an invention so rare and so little regarded, is given
by Adam Smith himself. Division of labour, as he points out,
is limited by the extent of the market, and, owing chiefly to bad
means of communication, the market for English manufactures
was still a very narrow one. Yet England, however slow the development of her manufactures, advanced nevertheless more rapidly in this respect than other nations. One great secret of her
progress lay in the facilities for water-carriage afforded by her
rivers, for all communication by land was still in the most neg-
lected condition. A second cause was the absence of internal
customs barriers, such as existed in France, and in Prussia until
Stein's time. The home trade of England was absolutely free.

Arthur Young gives abundant evidence of the execrable state
of the roads. It took a week or more for a coach to go from
London to Edinburgh. On 'that infernal' road between Preston
and Wigan the ruts were four feet deep, and he saw three carts
break down in a mile of road. At Warrington the turnpike was
'most infamously bad,' and apparently 'made with a view to immediate destruction.' 'Very shabby,' 'execrable,' 'vile,' 'most
execrably vile,' are Young's ordinary comments on the highways.
But the water routes for traffic largely made up for the defi-
ciencies of the land routes.

Attempts to improve water communication began with deepening the river beds. In 1635 there was a project for rendering
the Avon navigable from its junction with the Severn at Tewkes-
bury through Gloucestershire, Worcestershire, and Warwickshire,

but it was abandoned owing to the civil war. From 1660 to 1755 various Acts were passed for deepening the beds of rivers. In 1720 there was an Act for making the Mersey and Irwell navigable between Liverpool and Manchester. About the same time the navigation of the Aire and Calder was opened out. In 1755 the first canal was made, eleven miles in length, near Liverpool. Three years later the Duke of Bridgewater had another contructed from his coal mines at Worsley to Manchester, seven miles distant. Between 1761 and 1766 a still longer one of twenty-nine miles was completed from Manchester through Chester to the Mersey above Liverpool. From this time onwards the canal system spread with great rapidity.

When we turn to investigate the industrial organisation of the time, we find that the class of capitalist employers was as yet but in its infancy. A large part of our goods were still produced on the domestic system. Manufactures were little concentrated in towns, and only partially separated from agriculture. The 'manufacturer' was, literally, the man who worked with his own hands in his own cottage. Nearly the whole cloth trade of the West Riding, for instance, was organised on this system at the beginning of the century.

An important feature in the industrial organisation of the time was the existence of a number of small master-manufacturers, who were entirely independent, having capital and land of their own, for they combined the culture of small freehold pasture-farms with their handicraft. Defoe has left an interesting picture of their life. The land near Halifax, he says, was 'divided into small Enclosures from two Acres to six or seven each, seldom more, every three or four Pieces of Land had an House belonging to them; . . . hardly an House standing out of a Speaking-distance from another; . . . we could see at every House a Tenter, and on almost every Tenter a piece of Cloth or Kersie or Shaloon. . . . Every clothier keeps one horse, at least, to carry his Manufactures to the Market; and every one, generally, keeps a Cow or two or more for his Family. By this means the small Pieces of enclosed Land about each house are occupied, for they scarce sow Corn enough to feed their Poultry. . . . The houses are full of lusty Fellows, some at the Dye-vat, some at the looms, others dressing the Cloths; the women and children carding or spinning; being all employed from the youngest to the oldest. . . . Not a Beggar to be seen nor an idle person.'[26]

This system, however, was no longer universal in Arthur Young's time. That writer found at Sheffield a silk-mill employing 152 hands, including women and children; at Darlington 'one master-manufacturer employed above fifty looms'; at Boyton there were 150 hands in one factory.[27] So, too, in the West of England cloth-trade the germs of the capitalist system were visible. The rich merchant gave out work to labourers in the surrounding villages, who were his employés, and were not independent. In the Nottingham hosiery trade there were, in 1750 fifty manufacturers, known as 'putters out,' who employed 1200 frames; in Leicestershire 1800 frames were so employed.[28] In the hand-made nail business of Staffordshire and Worcestershire the merchant had warehouses in different parts of the district and give out nail-rod iron to the nail-master, sufficient for a week's work for him and his family.[29] In Lancashire we can trace, step by step, the growth of the capitalist employer. At first we see, as in Yorkshire, the weaver furnishing himself with warp and weft, which he worked up in his own house and brought himself to market. By degrees he found it difficult to get yarn from the spinners;[30] so the merchants at Manchester gave him out linen warp and raw cotton, and the weaver became dependent on them.[31] Finally, the merchant would get together thirty or forty looms in a town. This was the nearest approach to the capitalist system before the great mechanical inventions.

Coming to the system of exchange, we find it based on several different principles, which existed side by side, but which were all, as we should think, very simple and primitive. Each trade had its centre in a provincial town. Leeds, for instance, had its market twice a week, first on the bridge over the Aire, afterward in the High Street, where, at a later time, two halls were built. Every clothier had his stall, to which he would bring his cloth (seldom more than one piece at a time, owing to the frequency of the markets). At six or seven o'clock a bell rang, and the market began; the merchants and factors came in and made their bargains with the clothiers, and in little more than an hour the whole business was over. By nine the benches were cleared and the hall empty.[32] There was a similar hall at Halifax for the worsted trade. But a large portion of the inland traffic was carried on at fairs, which were still almost as important as in the Middle Ages. The most famous of all was the great fair of Sturbridge,[33] which lasted from the middle of August to the middle of September. Hither came representatives of all the great trades. The merchants of Lancashire brought their goods on a thousand pack-horses; the Eastern counties sent their worsteds, and Birmingham its hardware. An immense quantity of wool was sold, orders being taken by the wholesale dealers of London. In fact, a large part of the home trade found its way to this market.[34] There were also the four great annual fairs, which retained the ancient title of 'marts,' at Lynn, Boston, Gainsborough, and Beverley.[35]

The link between these fairs and the chief industrial centres was furnished by travelling merchants. Some would go from Leeds with droves of pack-horses to all the fairs and market-towns throughout England.[36] In the market-towns they sold to the shops; elsewhere they would deal directly with the consumer, like the Manchester merchants, who sent their pack-horses the round of the farmhouses, buying wool or other commodities in exchange for their finished goods. Sometimes the London merchants would come to the manufacturers, paying their guineas down at once, and taking away the purchases themselves. So too in the Birmingham lock trade, chapmen would go round with pack-horses to buy from manufacturers; in the brass trade likewise the manufacturer stayed at home, and the merchant came round with cash in his saddle-bags, and put the brasswork which he purchased into them, though in some cases he would order it to be sent by carrier.[37]

Ready cash was essential, for banking was very little developed. The Bank of England existed, but before 1759 issued no notes of less value than £20. By a law of 1709 no other bank of more than six partners was allowed; and in 1750, according to Burke, there were not more than 'twelve bankers' shops out of London.'[38] The Clearing-House was not established till 1775.

Hampered as the inland trade was by imperfect communications, extraordinary efforts were made to promote exchange. It is striking to find waste silk from London made into silk-yarn at Kendal and sent back again,[39] or cattle brought from Scotland to Norfolk to be fed.[40] Many districts, however, still remained completely excluded, so that foreign products never reached them at all. Even at the beginning of this century the Yorkshire yeoman, as described by Southey,[41] was ignorant of sugar, potatoes, and cotton; the Cumberland dalesman, as he appears in Wordsworth's *Guide to the Lakes*,[42] lived entirely on the produce of his farm. It was this domestic system which the great socialist writers Sismondi and Lassalle had in their minds when they inveighed against the modern organisation of industry. Those who lived under it, they pointed out, though poor, were on the whole prosperous; over-production was absolutely impossible.[43] Yet at the time of which I am speaking, many of the evils which modern Socialists lament were already visible, especially in those industries which produced for the foreign market. Already there were complaints of the competition of men who pushed themselves into the market to take advantage of high prices; already we hear of fluctuations of trade and irregularity of employment.[44] The old simple conditions of production and exchange were on the eve of disappearance before the all-corroding force of foreign trade.

The home trade was still indeed much greater in proportion than now; but the exports had grown from about £7,000,000 at the beginning of the century[45] to £14,500,000 in 1760. During that interval great changes had taken place in the channels of foreign commerce. In 1700 Holland was our great market, taking more than one-third of all our exports, but in 1760 the proportion was reduced to about one-seventh. Portugal, which in 1703 took one-seventh, now took only about one-twelfth. The trade with France was quite insignificant. On the other hand, the Colonies were now our chief markets, and a third of our exports went there. In 1770 America took three-fourths of all the manufactures of Manchester.[46] In 1767 the exports to Jamaica were nearly as great as they had been to all the English plantations together in 1704.[47] The shipping trade had doubled,[48] and the ships themselves were larger. In 1732 ships 750 tons were considered remarkable; in 1770 there were many in Liverpool of 900 tons; but in this as in other branches of business progress was still slow, partial, local, thus presenting a striking contrast to the rapid and general advance of the next half-century.

　　　　　　　ENGLAND IN 1760

The Decay of the Yeomanry

IT is a reflection that must have occurred to every one that the popular philosophy of the day, while in the region of speculation it has undermined ancient beliefs, has exerted in the practical world a distinctly conservative influence. The conception of slow development, according to definite laws, undoubtedly tends to strengthen the position of those who offer resistance to radical changes. It may, however, well be doubted whether the theory of evolution is really such a support as it seems to be to those who would uphold the existing framework of society. It is certainly remarkable that the most recent legislation has been at once revolutionary in its character and justified by appeals to historical experience. I do not forget that the most distinguished exponent of the doctrine of evolution as applied to politics has developed a theory of government opposed to recent legislative reforms, but that theory is an *a priori* one. Those, on the other hand, who have applied the historical method to political economy and the science of society, have shown an unmistakable disposition to lay bare the injustice to which the humbler classes of the community have been exposed, and to defend methods and institutions adopted for their protection which have never received scientific defence before.

The fact is, that the more we examine the actual course of affairs, the more we are amazed at the unnecessary suffering that has been inflicted upon the people. No generalities about natural law or inevitable development can blind us to the fact, that the progress in which we believe has been won at the expense of much injustice and wrong, which was not inevitable. Perhaps this is most conspicuous in our land system, and we shall find

EDITOR'S NOTE: The greater part of this chapter is taken from an essay in Toynbee's own handwriting.

with regard to it, as with regard to some other matters, that the more we accept the method of historical inquiry, the more revolutionary shall we tend to become in practice. For while the modern historical school of economists appear to be only exploring the monuments of the past, they are really shaking the foundations of many of our institutions in the present. The historical method is often deemed conservative, because it traces the gradual and stately growth of our venerable institutions; but it may exercise a precisely opposite influence by showing the gross injustice which was blindly perpetrated during this growth. The historical method is supposed to prove that economic changes have been the inevitable outcome of natural laws. It just as often proves them to have been brought about by the self-seeking action of dominant classes.

It is a singular thing that no historian has attempted an adequate explanation of the disappearance of the small freeholders who, down to the close of the seventeenth century, formed with their families one-sixth of the population of England, and whose stubborn determination enabled Cromwell and Fairfax to bring the Civil War to a successful close. This neglect is the more remarkable, as economists have so emphatically dwelt upon the extraordinary difference between the distribution of landed property in England and in countries like Germany and France. The modern reformer is content to explain the facts by the existence in England of a law of primogeniture and a system of strict settlement, but the explanation is obviously a superficial one. To show why in England the small landed proprietors have vanished, whilst in Germany and France they have increased and thriven, it is necessary to carry our inquiries far back into the history of law, politics, and commerce. The result of a closer examination of the question is a little startling, for we find that the present distribution of landed property in England is in the main due to the existence of the system of political government which has made us a free people. And on the other hand, the distribution of landed property in France and Germany, which writer after writer points to as the great bulwark against revolution, is in the main due to a form of government that destroyed political liberty and placed the people in subjection to the throne.

Evidence in support of this conclusion is not difficult to adduce. The first fact which arouses our interest is that at the conclusion of the seventeenth century it was estimated by Gregory King that there were 180,000 freeholders in England,[1] and that, less than a hundred years later, the pamphleteers of the time, and even careful writers like Arthur Young, speak of the small freeholders as practically gone. The bare statement of this contrast is in itself most impressive. A person ignorant of our history during the intervening period might surmise that a great exterminatory war had taken place, or a violent social revolution which had caused a transfer of the property of one class to another. But though the surmise in this particular form would be incorrect, we are nevertheless justified in saying that a revolution of incalculable importance had taken place,—a revolution, though so silent, of as great importance as the political revolution of 1831. 'The able and substantial freeholders,' described by Whitelock, 'the freeholders and freeholders' sons, well armed within with the satisfaction of their own good consciences, and without by iron arms, who stood firmly and charged desperately,'—this devoted class, who had broken the power of the king and the squires in the Civil Wars, were themselves, within a hundred years from that time, being broken, dispersed, and driven off the land. Numerous and prosperous in the fifteenth century, they had suffered something by the enclosures of the sixteenth; but though complaints are from time to time made in the seventeenth of the laying together of farms, there is no evidence to show that their number underwent any great diminution during that time. In the picture of country life which we find in the literature of the first years of the eighteenth century, the small freeholder is still a prominent figure. Sir Roger de Coverley, in riding to Quarter Sessions, points to the two yeomen who are riding in front of him, and Defoe, in his admirable *Tour through England,* first published a few years later, describes with satisfaction the number and prosperity of the Grey-coats of Kent (as they were called from their home-spun garments), whose political power forced the gentlemen to treat them with circumspection and deference.[2] 'Of the freeholders of England,' says Chamberlayne, in the *State of Great Britain*,[3] first published towards the close of the seventeenth century, 'there are more in number and richer than in any country of the like extent in Europe. £40 or £50 a year is very ordinary, £100 or £200 in some counties is not rare; sometimes in Kent, and in the Weald of Sussex, £500 or £600 per annum, and £3000 or £4000 stock.' The evidence is conclusive that up to the Revolution of 1688 the freeholders were in most parts of the country an important feature in social life.

If, however, we ask whether they had possessed, as a class, any political initiative, we must answer in the negative. In the lists of the Eastern Counties' Association, formed in the Civil War (the eastern counties were the districts, perhaps, where the freeholders were strongest), we find no name which has not appended to it the title of gentleman or esquire. The small landed proprietor, though courageous and independent in personal character, was ignorant, and incapable himself of taking the lead. There was litte to stimulate his mind in his country life; in agriculture he pursued the same methods as his forefathers, was full of prejudices, and difficult to move. The majority of this class had never travelled beyond their native village or homestead and the neighbouring market-town. In some districts those freeholders were also artisans, especially in the eastern counties, which were still the richest part of the country, and the most subject to foreign influence. But, on the whole, if we may judge from the accounts of rather later times, the yeomen, though thriving in good seasons, often lived very hard lives, and remained stationary in their habits and ways of thinking from generation to generation. They were capable in the Civil War, under good leadership, of proving themselves the most powerful body in the kingdom; but after constitutional government had been secured, and the great landowners were independent of their support, they sank into political insignificance. The Revolution of 1688, which brought to a conclusion the constitutional struggle of the seventeenth century, was accomplished without their aid, and paved the way for their extinction. A revolution in agricultural life was the price paid for political liberty.

At first, however, the absorption of the small freeholders went on slowly. The process of disappearance has been continuous from about 1700 to the present day, but it is not true to say, as Karl Marx does,[4] that the yeomanry had disappeared by the middle of the eighteenth century. It was not till the very period which we are considering, that is to say about 1760, that the process of extinction became rapid. There is conclusive evidence that many were still to be found about 1770. There were at that time still 9000 freeholders in Kent.[5]

Even as late as 1807, estates in Essex, if divided, were bought by farmers at high prices, and there was some prospect of landed property coming back to the conditions of a century before, 'when our inferior gentry resided upon their estates in the country'; and about the same date there were in Oxfordshire 'many proprietors of a middling size, and many small proprietors, particularly in the open fields.'[6] They were especially strong in Cumberland, the West Riding, and parts of the East Riding. In the Vale of Pickering in 1788 nearly the whole district belonged to them, and no great landowner had been able to get a footing.[7] But in 1788 this was already an exceptional case, and in other writers of that period we find a general lament at the disappearance of the yeoman. Arthur Young 'sincerely regrets the loss of that set of men who are called yeomen . . . who really kept up the independence of the nation,' and is 'loth to see their lands now in the hands of monopolising lords;'[8] and in 1787 he admits that they had practically disappeared from most parts of the country.[9] And with the yeomen went the small squires, victims of the same causes.[10]

These causes, as I stated above, are to be sought less in economical than in social and political facts. The chief of them was our peculiar form of government. After the Revolution the landed gentry were practically supreme. Not only national but local administration was entirely in their hands, and, as a natural consequence, land, being the foundation of social and political influence, was eagerly sought after. We may contrast France and Prussia, where the landowners had no political power as such, and where, in consequence, small properties remained un-assailed. The second fact is the enormous development of the mercantile and moneyed interest. The merchants could only obtain political power and social position by becoming landowners. It is true that Swift says that 'the power which used to follow land had gone over to money,' and that the great Turkey merchants, like Addison's Sir Andrew Freeport, occupied a good position; but few mere merchants were in Parliament,[11] and Dr. Johnson made the significant remark that 'an English merchant is a new species of gentleman.'[12] To make himself a gentleman, therefore, the merchant who had accumulated his wealth in the cities, which, as we have seen, were growing rapidly during the first half of the eighteenth century with an expanding commerce, bought land as a matter of course. Hence the mercantile origin of much of our nobility. James Lowther, created Earl of Lonsdale in 1784, was great-grandson of a Turkey merchant; the ancestor of the Barings was a clothier in Devonshire; Anthony Petty, father of Sir W. Petty, and the ancestor on the female side of the Petty-Fitzmaurices, was a clothier at Romsey, in Hampshire; Sir Josiah Child's son became Earl of Tilney.[13] The landowners in the West of England, 'who now,' in Defoe's words, 'carry their heads so high,' made their fortunes in the clothing trade. And not only did a new race of landowners thus spring up, but the old families enriched themselves, and so were enabled to buy more land by intermarriage with the commercial magnates. The Fitzmaurices, for instance, inherited the wealth of the Pettys: Child's daughter married the Marquis of Worcester, and, by a second marriage, Lord Grenville of Potheridge; Lord Conway and Walpole married daughters of John Shorter, merchant of London. 'I think I remember,' said Sir R. Temple between 1675 and 1700, 'the first noble families that married into the City for money.'[14] 'Trade,' said Defoe, 'is so far here from being inconsistent with a gentleman, that, in short, trade in England makes gentlemen; for, after a generation or two, the tradesmen's children, or at least their grandchildren, come to be as good gentlemen, statesmen, parliament-men, privy-councillors, judges, bishops, and noblemen, as those of the highest birth, and the most ancient families.' [15] Contrast this fusion of classes with the French society of the last century, with its impoverished nobility, living often on the seignorial rights and rent-charges of their alienated estates, but hardly ever intermarrying with the commercial classes; or that of Prussia, where the two classes remained entirely separate, and could not even purchase one another's land.

I have established two facts: the special reason for desiring land after the Revolution as a condition of political power and social prestige, and the means of buying land on the part of the wealthy merchants or of the nobility and greater gentry enriched by matrimonial alliances with the great commercial class. Now here is a piece of evidence to show that it was the accepted policy of the large landowners to buy out the yeoman. The land agent, whom I have so often quoted, lays down as a maxim for the model steward that he 'should not forget to make the best inquiry into the disposition of the freeholders, within or near any of his lord's manors, to sell their lands, that he may use his best endeavours to purchase them at as reasonable a price as may be for his lord's advantage and convenience.' [16]

On the other hand, as a result of the supremacy of the great landowners in Parliament, their own estates were artificially protected. The system of strict settlements, introduced by Sir Orlando Bridgman in 1666, though not so important as it is often made out to be, prevented much land from coming into the market, though it did not prevent merchants from buying when they wished. The custom of primogeniture checked the division of estates by leading to the disuse of inheritance by gavelkind, and similar customs. In Cumberland primogeniture was introduced among the freeholders in the sixteenth century; in Kent there was, in 1740, nearly as much gavelkind as before the disgavelling Acts began, but thirty years later it was being superseded by primogeniture. It was during these thirty years that the process of concentration in that county first assumed formidable proportions. In Pickering, on the other hand, where the law of equal division still held its own, small landowners also, as we have seen, survived after their extinction in most parts of England.

A third result of landlord supremacy was the manner in which the common-field system was broken up. Allusion has already been made to enclosures, and enclosures meant a break-up of the old system of agriculture and a redistribution of the land. This is a problem which involves delicate questions of justice. In Prussia, the change was effected by impartial legislation; in England, the work was done by the strong at the expense of the weak. The change from common to individual ownership, which was economically advantageous, was carried out in an iniquitous manner, and thereby became socially harmful. Great injury was thus done to the poor and ignorant freeholders who lost their rights in the common lands. In Pickering, in one instance, the lessee of the tithes applied for an enclosure of the waste. The small freeholders did their best to oppose him, but, having little money to carry on the suit, they were overruled, and the lessee, who had bought the support of the landless 'house-owners' of the parish, took the land from the freeholders and shared the spoil with the cottagers.[17] It was always easy for the steward to harass the small owners till he forced them to sell, like Addison's Touchy, whose income had been reduced by lawsuits from £80 to £30, though in this case it is true he had only himself to blame.[18] The enclosure of waste land, too, did great damage to the small freeholders, who, without the right of grazing, naturally found it so much the more difficult to pay their way.

Though the economical causes of the disappearance of the yeomen were comparatively unimportant, they served to accelerate the change. Small arable farms would not pay, and must, in any case, have been thrown together. The little farmers, according to Arthur Young, worked harder and were to all intents and purposes as low in the comforts of life as the day-labourers. But their wretchedness was entirely owing to their occupying arable instead of grass lands.[19] And apart from this, undoubtedly, the new class of large farmers were superior, in some respects, to the too unprogressive yeomen,—'quite a different sort of men . . . in point of knowledge and ideas,' [20] with whose improved methods of agriculture the yeomen found it difficult to compete. A further economic cause which tended to depress many of the yeomen was the gradual destruction of domestic industries, which injured them as it injures the German peasant at the present day. In Cumberland the yeomen began to disappear when the spinning-wheel was silenced.[21] The decay of the home manufacture of cloth seems to have considerably affected the Grey-coats of Kent. And finally, as the small towns and villages decayed, owing to the consolidation of farms and of industry, the small freeholders lost their market, for the badness of the roads made it difficult for them to send their produce far. Hence the small freeholders survived longest where they owned dairy-farms, as in Cumberland and the West Riding, and where domestic industry flourished, and they had a market for their products in their own neighbourhood.

When once the ranks of the yeomanry had been appreciably thinned, the process of extinction went on with ever-growing rapidity. The survivors became isolated. They would have no one of their own station to whom they could marry their daughters, and would become more and more willing to sell their lands, however strong the passion of possession might be in some places.[22] The more enterprising, too, would move off to the towns to make their fortunes there, just as at the present day the French peasants are attracted to the more interesting and exciting life of the town. Thus Sir Robert Peel's grandfather was originally a yeoman farming his own estate, but being of an inventive turn of mind he took to cotton manufacturing and printing.[23] This was particularly the case with the small squires, who grew comparatively poorer and poorer, and found it increasingly difficult to keep pace with the rise in the standard of comfort. Already, at the end of the seventeenth century, the complaint had been raised that the landowners were beginning to live in the county towns. Afterwards, the more wealthy came up to London; Sir Roger de Coverley had a house in Soho Square. The small country gentleman felt the contrast between him and his richer neighbours more and more; and as he had

none of the political power attaching to land—for the great
landowners had the whole administration in their hands—there
was every inducement for him to sell and invest his money in
a more profitable manner.

To summarise the movement: it is probable that the yeomen
would in any case have partly disappeared, owing to the inevitable working of economic causes. But these alone would
not have led to their disappearance on so large a scale. It was
the political conditions of the age, the overwhelming importance
of land, which made it impossible for the yeoman to keep his
grip upon the soil.

The Condition of the Wage-Earners

THE condition of the agricultural labourer had very much improved since the beginning of the century. In the seventeenth century his average daily wage had been 10¼d., while the average price of corn had been 38s. 2d. During the first sixty years of the eighteenth century his average wages were 1s., the price of corn 32s.[1] Thus, while the price of corn had, thanks to a succession of good seasons, fallen 16 per cent., wages had risen to about an equal extent, and the labourer was thus doubly benefited. Adam Smith attributes this advance in prosperity to 'an increase in the demand for labour, arising from the great and almost universal prosperity of the country';[2] but at the same time he allows that wealth had only advanced gradually, and with no great rapidity. The real solution is to be found in the slow rate of increase in the numbers of the people. Wealth had indeed grown slowly, but its growth had nevertheless been more rapid than that of population.

The improvement in the condition of the labourer was thus due to an increase in real and not only in nominal wages. It is true that certain articles, such as soap, salt, candles, leather, fermented liquors, had, chiefly owing to the taxes laid on them, become a good deal dearer, and were consumed in very small quantities; but the enhanced prices of these things were more than counterbalanced by the greater cheapness of grain, potatoes, turnips, carrots, cabbages, apples, onions, linen and woollen cloth, instruments made of the coarser metals, and household furniture.[3] Wheaten bread had largely superseded rye and barley bread, which were 'looked upon with a sort of horror,' wheat being as cheap as rye and barley had been in former times.[4] Every poor family drank tea once a day at least—a 'pernicious commodity,' a 'vile superfluity,' in Arthur Young's eyes.[5] Their consumption of meat was 'pretty considerable'; that of cheese was 'immense.' [6] In 1737 the day-labourers of England, 'by their large wages and cheapness of all necessaries,' enjoyed better dwellings, diet, and apparel in England, than the husbandmen or farmers did in other countries.' [7] The middle of the eighteenth century was indeed about his best time, though a decline soon set in. By 1771 his condition had already been somewhat affected by the dear years immediately preceding, when prices had risen much faster than wages, although the change had as yet, according to Young, merely cut off his superfluous expenditure.[8] By the end of the century men had begun to look back with regret upon this epoch in the history of the agricultural labourer as one of a vanished prosperity. At no time since the passing of the 43d of Elizabeth, wrote Eden in 1796, 'could the labouring classes acquire such a portion of the necessaries and conveniences of life by a day's work, as they could before the late unparalleled advance in the price of the necessaries of life.' [9]

Nor were high wages and cheap food their only advantages. Their cottages were often rent-free, being built upon the waste. Each cottage had its piece of ground attached,[10] though the piece was often a very small one, for the Act of Elizabeth, providing that every cottage should have four acres of land, was doubtless unobserved, and was repealed in 1775. Their common rights, besides providing fuel, enabled them to keep cows and pigs and poultry on the waste, and sheep on the fallows and stubbles. But these rights were already being steadily curtailed, and there was 'an open war against cottages,' [11] consequent on the tendency to consolidate holdings into large sheep-farms. It was becoming customary, too, for unmarried labourers to be boarded in the farmers' houses.

On the whole, the agricultural labourer, at any rate in the south of England, was much better off in the middle of the eighteenth century than his descendants were in the middle of the nineteenth. At the later date wages were actually lower in Suffolk, Essex, and perhaps parts of Wilts, than they were at the former; in Berks they were exactly the same; in Norfolk, Bucks, Gloucestershire, and South Wilts, there had been a very trifling rise; with the exception of Sussex and Oxfordshire, there was no county south of the Trent in which they had risen more than one-fourth.[12] Meanwhile rent and most necessaries, except bread, had increased enormously in cost, while most of the labourer's old privileges were lost, so that his real wages had actually diminished. But in the manufacturing districts of the north his condition had improved. While nominal wages in the south had risen on the average 14 per cent., here they had risen on the average 66 per cent. In some districts the rise had been as great as 200 per cent. In Arthur Young's time the agricultural wages of Lancashire were 4s. 6d.—the lowest rate in England; in 1821 they had risen to 14s. It may be roughly said that the relative positions of the labourer north and south of the Trent had been exactly reversed in the course of a century.

In Arthur Young's time the highest wages were to be found in Lincolnshire, the East Riding, and, following close upon these, the metropolitan and eastern counties. At first sight the high rate of wages in the first two counties seems to contradict the general law about their relative condition in north and south. But on investigation we find it to be due to exceptional circumstances. Arguing on the deductive method, we should conjecture a large demand for or a small supply of labour; and, in fact, we find both these influences in operation. The population had actually diminished, in Lincolnshire from 64 to 58 to the square mile, in the East Riding, from 80 to 71; this was partly due to the enclosures and the conversion of arable to pasture, partly to the increase of manufactures in the West Riding. Thus the labourers had been drawn off to the latter at the same time that they were being driven out of the agricultural districts. And for the remaining labourers there was a great demand in public works, such as turnpike-roads and agricultural improvements on a large scale.[13]

But there were many local variations of wages which are far less easy to bring under the ordinary rules of Political Economy. There was often the greatest inequality in the same county. In Lincolnshire, for instance, wages varied from 12s. 3d. to 7s., and even 6s.[14] It was at this very time that Adam Smith, arguing deductively from his primary axiom that men follow their pecuniary interest, enunciated the law that wages tend to an equality in the same neighbourhood and the same occupation. Why then these variations? Adam Smith himself partly supplies the answer. His law pretends to exactness only 'when society is left to the natural course of things.' [15] Now this was impossible when natural tendencies were diverted by legal restrictions on the movement of labour, such as the law of settlement, which re-sulted in confining every labourer to his own parish. But we must not seek the cause of these irregularities of wages merely in legal restrictions. Apart from disturbing influences such as this, men do not always act in accordance with their pecuniary in-terest; there are other influences at work affecting their conduct. One of the strongest of these is attachment to locality. It was this influence which partly frustrated the recent efforts of the Labourers' Union to remove the surplus labour of the east and south to the north. Again, there are apathy and ignorance, factors of immense importance in determining the action of the uneducated majority of men. In 1872 there were labourers in Devon who had never heard of Lancashire, where they might have been earning double their own wages.[16] Human beings, as Adam Smith says, are 'of all baggage the most difficult to be transported,' [17] though their comparative mobility depends upon the degree of their education, the state of communications, and the industrial conditions of any particular time. The English labourer to-day is far more easy to move than he was a hundred years ago. In a stirring new country like America there is much more mobility of labour than in England.

Turning from the agricultural wage-earners to those engaged in manufactures, we find their condition at this period on the whole much inferior to what it is now. In spite of the widening gulf between capitalist and labourer, the status of the artisan has distinctly improved since Adam Smith's time. His nominal wages have doubled or trebled. A carpenter then earned 2s. 6d. a day; he now earns 5s. 6d. A cotton weaver then earned 5s.[18] a week, he now earns 20s., and so on. But it is difficult to compare the condition of the artisan as a whole at the two periods, because so many entirely new classes of workmen have come into existence during the past century; for instance, the engineers, whose Union now includes 50,000 men earning from 25s. to 40s. a week. And if wages have on the whole very greatly increased, there were, on the other hand, some obvious advantages which the artisan possessed in those days, but has since lost. For the manufacturing population still lived to a very great extent in the country. The artisan often had his small piece of land, which supplied him with wholesome food and healthy recreation. His wages and employment too were more regular. He was not subject to the uncertainties and knew nothing of the fearful sufferings which his descendants were to endure from commercial fluctuations, especially before the introduction of free trade. For the whole inner life of industry was, as we have seen, entirely different from what it now is. The relation between the workmen and their employers was much closer, so that in many industries they were not two classes but one. As among the agriculturists the farmer and labourer lived much the same life—for the capitalist farmers as a class were not yet in existence—and ate at the same board, so in manufacturing industries the journeyman was often on his way to become a master. The distribution of wealth was, indeed, in all respects more equal. Landed property, though gradually being concentrated, was still in a far larger number of hands, and even the great landlords possessed nothing like their present riches. They had no vast mineral wealth, or rapidly developing town property. A great number of the trading industries, too, were still in the hands of small capitalists. Great trades, like the iron trade, requiring large capital, had hardly come into existence.

VII THE MERCANTILE SYSTEM AND ADAM SMITH

THE contrast between the industrial England of 1760 and the industrial England of to-day is not only one of external conditions. Side by side with the revolution which the intervening century has effected in the methods and organisation of production, there has taken place a change no less radical in men's economic principles, and in the attitude of the State to individual enterprise. England in 1760 was still to a great extent under the mediæval system of minute and manifold industrial regulations. That system was indeed decaying, but it had not yet been superseded by the modern principle of industrial freedom. To understand the origin of the mediæval system we must go back to a time when the State was still conceived of as a religious institution with ends that embraced the whole of human life. In an age when it was deemed the duty of the State to watch over the individual citizen in all his relations, and provide not only for his protection from force and fraud, but for his eternal welfare, it was but natural that it should attempt to insure a legal rate of interest, fair wages, honest wares. Things of vital importance to man's life were not to be left to chance or self-interest to settle. For no philosophy had as yet identified God and Nature: no optimistic theory of the world had reconciled public and private interest. And at the same time, the smallness of the world and the community, and the comparative simplicity of the social system made the attempt to regulate the industrial relations of men less absurd than it would appear to us in the present day.

This theory of the State, and the policy of regulation and restriction which sprang from it, still largely affected English industry at the time when Adam Smith wrote. There was, indeed, great freedom of internal trade; there were no provincial customs-barriers as in contemporary France and Prussia. Adam Smith singled out this fact as one of the main causes of English prosperity, and to Colbert and Stein, and other admirers of the English system, such freedom appeared as an ideal to be constantly striven after. But though internal trade was free for the passage of commodities, yet there still existed a network of restrictions on the mobility of labour and capital. By the law of apprenticeship[1] no person could follow any trade till he had served his seven years. The operation of the law was limited, it is true, to trades already established in the fifth year of Elizabeth, and obtained only in market-towns and cities. But wherever there was a municipal corporation, the restrictions which they imposed made it generally impossible for a man to work unless he was a freeman of the town, and this he could as a rule become only by serving his apprenticeship. Moreover, the corporations supervised the prices and qualities of wares. In the halls, where the smaller manufacturers sold their goods, all articles exposed for sale were inspected. The mediæval idea still obtained that the State should guarantee the genuineness of wares: it was not left to the consumer to discover their quality. And in the Middle Ages, no doubt, when men used the same things from year to year, a proper supervision did secure good work. But with the expansion of trade it ceased to be effective. Sir Josiah Child already recognised that changes of fashion must prove fatal to it, and that a nation which intended to have the trade of the world must make articles of every quality.[2] Yet the belief in the necessity of regulation was slow in dying out, and fresh Acts to secure it were passed as late as George ii.'s reign.

It is not clear how far the restrictions on the mobility of capital and labour were operative. No doubt they succeeded to a large extent; but when Adam Smith wrote his bitter criticism of the corporations,[3] he was probably thinking of the particular instance of Glasgow, where Watt was not allowed to set up trade. There were, however, even at that time, many free towns, like Birmingham and Manchester, which flourished greatly from the fact of their freedom. And even in the chartered towns, if Eden is to be trusted, the restrictions were far less stringent than we should gather from Adam Smith.[4] 'I am persuaded,' he says, 'that a shoemaker, who had not served an apprenticeship, might exercise his industry at Bristol or Liverpool, with as little hazard of being molested by the corporation of either place, as of being disturbed by the borough-reve of Manchester or the head-constable at Birmingham.' Then after quoting and criticising Adam Smith, he adds: 'I confess, I very much doubt whether there is a single corporation in England, the exercise of whose rights does at present operate in this manner. . . . In this instance, as in many others, the insensible progress of society has reduced chartered rights to a state of inactivity.'[5] We may probably conclude that nonfreemen were often unmolested, but that, when trade was bad, they were liable to be expelled.

Another relic of Mediævalism was the regulation of wages by Justices of the Peace, a practice enjoined by the Act of Elizabeth already referred to. Adam Smith speaks of it as part of a general system of oppression of the poor by the rich. Whatever may have been the case in some instances this was not generally true. The country gentry were, on the whole, anxious to do justice to the working classes. Combinations of labourers were forbidden by law, because it was thought to be the wrong way of obtaining the object in view, not from any desire to keep down wages. The Justices often ordained a rise in wages, and the workmen themselves were strongly in favour of this method of fixing them. The employers on their part also often approved of it. In fact we have an exactly similar system at the present day in boards of arbitration. The Justice was an arbitrator, appointed by law; and it is a mistaken assumption that such authoritative regulation may not have been good in its day.

The principle of regulation was applied much more thoroughly to our external than to our internal trade. The former was entirely carried on by great chartered companies, whether they were on a joint-stock footing, like the East India Company, or were 'regulated' like the Turkey Company, in which every man traded on his own Capital.[6] Here, again, Adam Smith carried too far his revolt against the restrictive system, which led him to denounce corporate trading as vicious in principle. 'The directors of such companies,' he says, 'being the managers rather of other people's money than of their own, it cannot well be expected that they should watch over it with the same anxious vigilance with which the partners in a private copartnery frequently watch over their own. . . . Negligence and profusion must always prevail, more or less, in the management of the affairs of such a company.'[7] This is an instance of pure *a priori* reasoning, but Smith's main argument is derived from the history of Joint-Stock Companies. He sought to show that, as a matter of fact, unless they had had a monopoly, they had failed; that is, he proceeded inductively, and wound up with an empirical law: 'it seems *contrary to all experience* that a Joint-Stock Company should be able to carry on successfully any branch of foreign trade, when private adventurers can come into any sort of open and fair competition with them.'[8] But he was too honest not to admit exceptions to his rule, as in the instance of banking, which he explained by the fact that it could be reduced to routine.

Smith's empirical law is, as we all now know, far from being universally true, though it was a reasonable induction enough at the time when it was made. Since then a large number of Joint-Stock Companies have succeeded, as for instance in the iron trade. Nor is it difficult to see the reason of this change. The habit of combination is stronger than it was, and we have discovered how to interest paid servants by giving them a share in the results of the enterprises they direct. Experience has shown also that a big company can buy the best brains. In the recent depression of trade the ironworks of Dowlais, which are managed on the Joint-stock system, alone remained successful amid many surrounding failures, and that because they had the ablest man in the district as manager.

In Adam Smith's time, however, the existence of Joint-Stock Companies was due not to any notion of their economical superiority, but to the tendency to place restrictions upon individual enterprise, based upon that belief in the antagonism of public and private interests which was characteristic of the time. The same idea of opposition obtained equally in international relations. The prosperity of one country was thought to be incompatible with that of another. If one profited by trade, it seemed to do so at the expense of its neighbours. This theory was the foundation of the mercantile system. It had its origin in the spirit of Nationalism—the idea of self-sustained and complete national life—which came in with the Renaissance and the Reformation.

But how came this Nationalism to be connected with a belief in the special importance of gold and silver, which is generally regarded as the essence of the mercantile system? The object of that system was national greatness, but national greatness depends on national riches generally, not on one particular kind of riches only, such as coin. The explanation must be sought in the fact that, owing to the simultaneous development of trade and the money system, gold and silver became peculiarly essential to the machinery of commerce. With the growth of standing armies, moreover, State finance acquired a new importance, and the object of State finance was to secure a ready supply of the precious metals. Thus the theory sprang up that gold and silver were the most solid and durable parts of the moveable wealth of a nation, and that, as they had more value in use than any other commodities, every state should do all in its power to acquire a great store of them. At first the Government tried to attain this object by accumulating a hoard; but this policy soon proved too wasteful and difficult. It then turned its attention to increasing the quantity of bullion in the hands of the people, for it came to see that if there was plenty of bullion in the country it could always draw upon it in case of need. The export of gold and silver was accordingly forbidden; but if hoarding had proved impracticable, this new method of securing the desired end was soon found to be useless, as the prohibition could be easily evaded. In the last resort, therefore, it was sought to insure a continuous influx of the precious metals through the ordinary channels of trade. If we bought less than we sold, it was argued, the balance of trade must be paid in coin. To accomplish this end every encouragement was given to the importation of raw materials and the necessaries of life, but the purchase of foreign manufactures was, for the most part, prohibited, and individuals were entreated not to buy imported luxuries. The result was retaliation abroad, and a deadlock in the commercial machine. Wars of tariff were common; for instance, we prohibited the importation of gold-lace from Flanders, and the Flemings in return excluded our wool. The system, however, resisted the teaching of experience, despite the fact that in abolishing the prohibition of the export of gold and silver, the Government acknowledged the true principle of free trade put forward by the East Indian Company. The latter contended that the law forbidding the export of bullion was not only useless, since it was easily stultified by smuggling, but even, if enforced, was hurtful, since the Orientals would only sell their valuable goods for silver. The success of this contention marks the transition from the Mercantile System proper to modern Protection. The advocates of that system had shifted their ground, and instead of seeking merely to prohibit the export of the precious metals, they established a general protection of native industries.

Their measures were not all alike bad. The Navigation Acts, for instance, were defended by Adam Smith, and Mill has indorsed his defence, on the ground that national defence is more important than national opulence.[9]

The most famous of these Acts was the law of 1651,[10] by which no goods of the growth or manufacture of Asia, Africa, or America were to be imported into England, Ireland, or the Plantations, except in ships belonging to English subjects, and manned by a crew three-fourths of whom were English; while no goods of any country in Europe were to be imported except in English ships, or ships belonging to the country from which the goods came. The argument used by the promoters of the law was that by excluding the Dutch from the carrying trade to this country we should throw it into the hands of English shipowners, and there would be an increase of English ships. It was admitted, indeed, that this would be giving a monopoly to English shipowners and English sailors, and that therefore freights would be dearer, and a check given to the growth of commerce. It was further admitted that owing to their higher charges English ships might be driven out of neutral ports; but the contention was, that we should secure to ourselves the whole of the carrying trade between America and the West Indies and England, and that this would amply compensate for our expulsion from other branches of commerce.

These anticipations were on the whole fulfilled. The price of freights was raised, because English ships cost more to build and man than Dutch ships, and thus the total amount of our trade was diminished.[11] We were driven out of neutral ports, and lost the Russian and the Baltic trades, because the English shipowners, to whom we had given a monopoly, raised their charge.[12] But on the other hand, we monopolised the trade to ports coming within the scope of the Act, the main object of which was 'the preservation of our plantation trade entire.'[13] Our shipping received a great stimulus, and our maritime supremacy grew with it. At the time when the Navigation Act was passed our colonial trade was insignificant; New York and Jersey were Dutch; Georgia, the Carolinas, Pennsylvania, Nova Scotia were not yet planted; Virginia, Maryland, New England were in their infancy.[14] At the end of the century the Barbados alone employed 400 vessels; while with the growth of the colonies the English power at sea had increased, until it rivalled the Dutch. In the next century the continuous development of the American and East Indian trades gave us a position of unquestionable maritime superiority.[15]

There is another argument in favour of Protection, at any rate in its early days. Its stimulus helped to overcome the apathy and dulness of a purely agricultural population, and draw a part of the people into trade.[16] But here, as everywhere, Protection involves this great disadvantage, that, once given, it is difficult to withdraw, and thus in the end more harm is done than good. English industries would not have advanced so rapidly without Protection, but the system, once established, led to perpetual wrangling on the part of rival industries, and sacrificed India and the colonies to our great manufacturers. And our national dislike to Protection deepens into repugnance when we examine the details of the system. Looking at its results during the period from 1688 to 1776, when it was in full force, we are forced to acknowledge that Adam Smith's invectives against the merchants, violent as they were, were not stronger than the facts demanded.

But the maintenance of Protection cannot be entirely set down to the merchants. Though the trading classes acquired much influence at the Revolution, the landed gentry were still supreme in Parliament; and the question arises, why they should have lent themselves to a policy which in many cases, as in the prohibition of the export of wool, was distinctly opposed to the interests of agriculture. Adam Smith's explanation is very simple. The country gentleman, who was naturally 'least subject of all people to the wretched spirit of monopoly,' was imposed upon by the 'clamours and sophistry of merchants and manufacturers,' and 'the sneaking arts of underling tradesmen,' who persuaded him into a simple but honest conviction that their interest and not his was the interest of the public.[17] Now this is true, but it is not the whole truth. The landowners, no doubt, thought it their duty to protect trade, and, not understanding its details, they implicitly followed the teaching of the merchants. But, besides this, there was the close connection, already referred to, between them and the commercial classes. Their younger sons often went into trade; they themselves, in many cases, married merchants' daughters. Nor did they give their support gratuitously; they wanted Protection for themselves, and if they acquiesced in the prohibition of the wool export, they persuaded the merchants to allow them in return a bounty of 5s. a quarter on the export of corn.

One of the worst features of the system was the struggle of rival interests at home. A great instance of this was the war between the woollen and cotton trades, in which the former, supported by the landed interest,[18] for a long time had the upper hand, so that an excise duty was placed on printed calicoes, and in 1721 they were forbidden altogether. It was not till 1774 that they were allowed again, and the excise duty was not repealed till 1831. To take another instance: it was proposed in Parliament in 1750 to allow the importation of pig and bar iron from the colonies. The tanners at once petitioned against it, on the ground that if American iron was imported, less iron would be smelted in England, fewer trees would be cut down, and therefore their own industry would suffer; and the owners of woodland tracts supported the tanners, lest the value of their timber should be affected.[19] These are typical examples of the way in which, under a protective system, politics are complicated and degraded by the intermixture of commercial interests. And the freer a government is, and the more exposed to pressure on the part of its subjects, the worse will be the result. As an American observer has lately said, Protection may be well enough under a despotism, but in a republic it can never be successful.

We find still stronger illustration of the evils of Protection in our policy towards Ireland and the colonies. After the Cromwellian settlement, there had been an export of Irish cattle into England; 'but for the pacifying of our landed gentlemen,'[20] after the Restoration the import of Irish live stock, meat and dairy produce was prohibited from 1660 to 1685. As cattle-farming then became unprofitable, the Irish turned their lands into sheepwalks, and not only exported wool, but started woollen manufactures at home. Immediately a law was passed (1699) confining the export of Irish wool to the English market; and this was followed by the imposition of prohibitive duties on their woollen manufactures. The English manufacturers argued that as Ireland was protected by England, and its prosperity was due to English capital, the Irish ought to reconcile themselves to restrictions on their trade, in the interests of Englishmen. Besides, the joint interests of both kingdoms would be best considered if England and Ireland respectively monopolised the woollen and linen industries, and the two nations thus became dependent on one another. If we turn to the colonies, we find them regarded simply as markets and farms of the mother country. The same argument was used: that they owed everything to England, and therefore it was no tyranny to exploit them in her interests. They were, therefore, not allowed to export or import in any but British vessels; they might not export such commodities as Englishmen wanted to any part of Europe other than Great Britain;

while those of their raw materials in which our landowners feared competition were excluded from the English markets. All imports into the colonies from other parts of Europe, except Great Britain, were forbidden, in order that our manufacturers might monopolise the American market. Moreover, every attempt was made to prevent them from starting any manufactures at home. At the end of the seventeenth century some Americans had set on foot a woollen industry; in 1719 it was suppressed; all iron manufactures—even nail-making—were forbidden; a flourishing hat manufacture had sprung up, but at the petition of English hatters, these competitors were not allowed to export to England, or even from one colony to another. Adam Smith might well say, that 'to found a great empire, for the sole purpose of raising up a people of customers, may at first sight appear a project fit only for a nation of shopkeepers.'[21] Nothing contributed more than this commercial system to the Declaration of Independence, and it is significant that the same year which saw its promulgation saw also the publication of the *Wealth of Nations*.

Many people on first reading the *Wealth of Nations* are disappointed. They come to it expecting lucid arguments, the clear exposition of universal laws; they find much tedious and confused reasoning and a mass of facts of only temporary interest. But these very defects contributed to its immediate success. It was because Adam Smith examined in detail the actual conditions of the age, and wrote a handbook for the statesman, and not merely, as Turgot did, a systematised treatise for the philosopher, that he appealed so strongly to the practical men of his time, who, with Pitt, praised his 'extensive knowledge of detail,' as well as 'the depth of his philosophical research.' It was the combination of the two which gave him his power. He was the first great writer on the subject; with him political economy passed from the exchange and the market-place to the professor's study; but he was only groping his way, and we cannot expect to meet with neat arrangement and scientific precision of treatment in his book. His language is tentative, he sometimes makes distinctions which he forgets elsewhere, as was inevitable before the language of economics had been fixed by endless verbal discussions. He had none of Ricardo's power of abstract reasoning. His gift lay in the extent and quickness of his observation, and in his wonderful felicity of illustration. We study him because in him, as in Plato, we come into contact with a great original mind, which teaches us how to think and work.

Original people always are confused because they are feeling their way.

If we look for the fundamental ideas of Adam Smith, those which distinguish him most clearly from earlier writers, we are first struck by his cosmopolitanism. He was the precursor of Cobden in his belief that commerce is not of one nation, but that all the nations of the world should be considered as one great community. We may see how widely he had departed from the old national system of economy, by contrasting the mere title of his book, *The Wealth of Nations,* with that of Mun's treatise, *England's Treasure in Foreign Trade.* This cosmopolitanism necessitated a detailed refutation of the mercantile system. He had to prove that gold and silver were not more important than other forms of wealth; and that if we wanted to buy them, we could always do so, if we had other consumable goods to offer in exchange. But it might be objected: 'What if a nation refuses to take your other goods, and wants your gold?' Adam Smith replied: 'In that case, gold will leave your country and go abroad; as a consequence, prices will fall at home, foreigners will be attracted by the low prices to buy in your markets, and thus the gold will return.' I can give you an actual example from recent history to prove the truth of his deduction. During the potato famine of 1847, we had to import enormous quantities of grain from America, and as a consequence had to send there £16,000,-000 worth of bullion. Immediately prices rose in America and fell in England, English merchants discontinued buying in America, while American merchants bought largely in England, so that in the following year all the gold came back again.

Equally prominent in Adam Smith is his individualism, his complete and unhesitating trust in individual self-interest. He was the first to appeal to self-interest as a great bond of society.

As a keen observer, he could point to certain facts, which seemed to bear out his creed. If we once grant the principle of the division of labour, then it follows that one man can live only by finding out what other men want; it is on this fact, for instance, that the food supply of London depends. This is the basis of the doctrine of *laisser faire*. It implies competition, which would result, so Adam Smith believed, in men's wants being supplied at a minimum of cost. In upholding competition he was radically opposed to the older writers, who thought it a hateful thing; but his conclusion was quite true. Again it implies the best possible distribution of industry; for under a system of free competition, every man will carry on his trade in the locality most suitable for it.

But the principle of *laisser faire* breaks down in certain points not recognised by Adam Smith. It fails, for instance, in assuming that it is the interest of the producer to supply the wants of the consumer in the best possible manner, that it is the interest of the producer to manufacture honest wares. It is quite true that this is his interest, where the trade is an old-established one and has a reputation to maintain, or where the consumer is intelligent enough to discover whether a commodity is genuine or not. But these conditions exist only to a small extent in modern commerce. The trade of the present day is principally carried on with borrowed capital; and it may be a clever man's interest to sell as large a quantity of goods as possible in a few years and then throw up his business. Thus the interests of producer and consumer conflict, and it has been found necessary to pass Adulteration Acts, which recognise the non-identity of interest of seller and buyer. It was argued, indeed, in Parliament, when these acts were proposed, that consumers ought to take care of themselves, but the consumers are far too ignorant to do so, especially the poor who are the great consumers of the articles protected against adulteration. Adam Smith, moreover, could not foresee that internal free trade might result in *natural* monopolies. A conspicuous feature of our times is the concentration of certain industries in the hands of a few great capitalists, especially in America, where such rings actually dictate the prices of the market. Eighty-five per cent. of the Pennsylvania coal-mines, for instance, are in the hands of six or seven companies who act in combination. The easiest remedy for such monopolies would be international free trade; with international competition few could be maintained. Finally, in the distribution of wealth there must necessarily be a permanent antagonism of interests. Adam Smith himself saw this, when he said that the rate of wages depended on contracts between two parties whose interests were not identical. This being granted, we see that in distribution the 'harmony' of the individual and the public good is a figment. At the present day each class of workmen cares only for the wages of its own members. Hence the complete breakdown of the *laisser faire* system in the question of wages. We have been driven to attempt the establishment of Boards of Conciliation all over the country, thus virtually surrendering the principle. Nor is it true that self-interest tends to supply all our wants; some of our best institutions, such as hospitals, owe their existence to altruistic sentiment.[22] These antagonisms were to come out more strongly than ever after Adam Smith's time. There were dark patches even in his age, but we now approach a darker period—a period as disastrous and as terrible as any through which a nation ever passed; disastrous and terrible, because, side by side with a great increase of wealth was seen an enormous increase of pauperism; and production on a vast scale, the result of free competition, led to a rapid alienation of classes and to the degradation of a large body of producers.

VIII   THE CHIEF FEATURES OF THE REVOLUTION

THE essence of the Industrial Revolution is the substitution of competition for the mediæval regulations which had previously controlled the production and distribution of wealth. On this account it is not only one of the most important facts of English history, but Europe owes to it the growth of two great systems of thought—Economic Science, and its antithesis, Socialism. The development of Economic Science in England has four chief landmarks, each connected with the name of one of the four great English economists. The first is the publication of Adam Smith's *Wealth of Nations* in 1776, in which he investigated the causes of wealth and aimed at the substitution of industrial freedom for a system of restriction. The production of wealth, not the welfare of man, was what Adam Smith had primarily before his mind's eye; in his own words, 'the great object of the Political Economy of every country is to increase the riches and power of that country.'[1] His great book appeared on the eve of the Industrial Revolution. A second stage in the growth of the science is marked by Malthus's *Essay on Population,* published in 1798, which may be considered the product of that revolution, then already in full swing. Adam Smith had concentrated all his attention on a large production; Malthus directed his inquiries, not to the causes of wealth but to the causes of poverty, and found them in his theory of population. A third stage is marked by Ricardo's *Principles of Political Economy and Taxation,* which appeared in 1817, and in which Ricardo sought to ascertain the laws of the distribution of wealth. Adam Smith had shown how wealth could be produced under a system of industrial freedom, Ricardo showed how wealth is distributed under such a system, a problem which could not have occurred to any one before his time. The fourth stage is marked by John

Stuart Mill's *Principles of Political Economy*, published in 1848. Mill himself asserted that 'the chief merit of his treatise' was the distinction drawn between the laws of production and those of distribution, and the problem he tried to solve was, how wealth *ought to be* distributed. A great advance was made by Mill's attempt to show what was and what was not inevitable under a system of free competition. In it we see the influence which the rival system of Socialism was already beginning to exercise upon the economists. The whole spirit of Mill's book is quite different from that of any economic works which had up to his time been written in England. Though a re-statement of Ricardo's system, it contained the admission that the distribution of wealth is the result of 'particular social arrangements,' and it recognised that competition alone is not a satisfactory basis of society.

Competition, heralded by Adam Smith, and taken for granted by Ricardo and Mill, is still the dominant idea of our time; though since the publication of the *Origin of Species,* we hear more of it under the name of the 'struggle for existence.' I wish here to notice the fallacies involved in the current arguments on this subject. In the first place it is assumed that all competition is a competition for existence. This is not true. There is a great difference between a struggle for mere existence and a struggle for a particular kind of existence. For instance, twelve men are struggling for employment in a trade where there is only room for eight; four are driven out of that trade, but they are not trampled out of existence. A good deal of competition merely decides what kind of work a man is to do;[2] though of course when a man can only do one kind of work, it may easily become a struggle for bare life. It is next assumed that this struggle for existence is a law of nature, and that therefore all human interference with it is wrong. To that I answer that the whole meaning of civilisation is interference with this brute struggle. We intend to modify the violence of the fight, and to prevent the weak being trampled under foot.

Competition, no doubt, has its uses. Without competition no progress would be possible, for progress comes chiefly from without; it is external pressure which forces men to exert themselves. Socialists, however, maintain that this advantage is gained at the expense of an enormous waste of human life and labour, which might be avoided by regulation. But here we must distinguish between competition in production and competition in distribution, a difference recognised in modern legislation, which has widened the sphere of contract in the one direction, while it has narrowed it in the other. For the struggle of men to outvie one another in production is beneficial to the community; their struggle over the division of the joint produce is not. The stronger side will dictate its own terms; and as a matter of fact, in the early days of competition the capitalists used all their power to oppress the labourers, and drove down wages to starvation point. This kind of competition has to be checked; there is no historical instance of its having lasted long without being modified either by combination or legislation, or both. In England both remedies are in operation, the former through Trades-Unions, the latter through factory legislation. In the past other remedies were applied. It is this desire to prevent the evils of competition that affords the true explanation of the fixing of wages by Justices of the Peace, which seemed to Ricardo a remnant of the old system of tyranny in the interests of the strong. Competition, we have now learnt, is neither good nor evil in itself; it is a force which has to be studied and controlled; it may be compared to a stream whose strength and direction have to be observed, that embankments may be thrown up within which it may do its work harmlessly and beneficially. But at the period we are considering it came to be believed in as a gospel, and, the idea of necessity being superadded, economic laws deduced from the assumption of universal unrestricted competition were converted into practical precepts, from which it was regarded as little short of immoral to depart.

Coming to the facts of the Industrial Revolution, the first thing that strikes us is the far greater rapidity which marks the growth of population. Before 1751 the largest decennial increase, so far as we can calculate from our imperfect materials, was 3 per cent. For each of the next three decennial periods the increase was 6 per cent.; then between 1781 and 1791 it was 9 per cent.; between 1791 and 1801, 11 per cent.; between 1801 and 1811, 14 per cent.; between 1811 and 1821, 18 per cent.[3] This is the highest figure ever reached in England, for since 1815 a vast emigration has been always tending to moderate it; between 1815 and 1880 over eight millions (including Irish) have left our shores. But for this our normal rate of increase would be 16 or 18 instead of 12 per cent. in every decade.[4]

Next we notice the relative and positive decline in the agricultural population. In 1811 it constituted 35 per cent. of the whole population of Great Britain; in 1821, 33 per cent.; in 1831, 28 per cent.[5] And at the same time its actual numbers have decreased. In 1831 there were 1,243,057 adult males employed in agriculture in Great Britain; in 1841 there were 1,207,989. In 1851 the whole number of persons engaged in agriculture in England was 2,084,153; in 1861 it was 2,010,454, and in 1871 it was 1,657,138.[6] Contemporaneously with this change, the centre of density of population has shifted from the Midlands to the North; there are at the present day 458 persons to the square mile in the counties north of the Trent, as against 312 south of the Trent. And we have lastly to remark the change in the relative population of England and Ireland. Of the total population of the three kingdoms, Ireland had in 1821 32 per cent., in 1881 only 14.6 per cent.

An agrarian revolution plays as large part in the great industrial change of the end of the eighteenth century as does the revolution in manufacturing industries, to which attention is more usually directed. Our next inquiry must therefore be: What were the agricultural changes which led to this noticeable decrease in the rural population? The three most effective causes were: the destruction of the common-field system of cultivation; the enclosure, on a large scale, of common and waste lands; and the consolidation of small farms into large. We have already seen that while between 1710 and 1760 some 300,000 acres were enclosed, between 1760 and 1843 nearly 7,000,000 underwent the same process. Closely connected with the enclosure system was the substitution of large for small farms. In the first half of the century Laurence, though approving of consolidation from an economic point of view, had thought that the odium attaching to an evicting landlord would operate as a strong check upon it.[7] But these scruples had now disappeared. Eden in 1795 notices how constantly the change was effected, often accompanied by the conversion of arable to pasture; and relates how in a certain Dorsetshire village he found two farms where twenty years ago there had been thirty.[8] The process went on uninterruptedly into the present century. Cobbett, writing in 1826, says: 'In the parish of Burghclere one single farmer holds, under Lord Carnarvon, as one farm, the lands that those now living remember to have formed fourteen farms, bringing up in a respectable way fourteen families.'[9] The consolidation of farms reduced the number of farmers, while the enclosures drove the labourers off the land, as it became impossible for them to exist without their rights of pasturage for sheep and geese on common lands.

Severely, however, as these changes bore upon the rural population, they wrought, without doubt, distinct improvement from an agricultural point of view. They meant the substitution of scientific for unscientific culture. 'It has been found,' says Laurence, 'by long experience, that common or open fields are great hindrances to the public good, and to the honest improvement which every one might make of his own.' Enclosures brought an extension of arable cultivation and the tillage of inferior soils; and in small farms of 40 to 100 acres, where the land was exhausted by repeated corn crops, the farm buildings of clay and mud walls and three-fourths of the estate often saturated with water,[10] consolidation into farms of 100 to 500 acres meant rotation of crops, leases of nineteen years, and good farm buildings. The period was one of great agricultural advance; the breed of cattle was improved, rotation of crops was generally introduced, the steam-plough was invented, agricultural societies were instituted.[11] In one respect alone the change was injurious. In consequence of the high prices of corn which prevailed during the French war, some of the finest permanent pastures were broken up. Still, in spite of this, it was said in 1813 that during the previous ten years agricultural produce had increased by one-fourth, and this was an increase upon a great increase in the preceding generation.[12]

Passing to manufactures, we find here the all-prominent fact to be the substitution of the factory for the domestic system, the consequence of the mechanical discoveries of the time. Four great inventions altered the character of the cotton manufacture; the spinning-jenny, patented by Hargreaves in 1770; the water-frame, invented by Arkwright the year before; Crompton's mule introduced in 1779, and the self-acting mule, first invented by Kelly in 1792, but not brought into use till Roberts improved it in 1825.[13] None of these by themselves would have revolution-ised the industry. But in 1769—the year in which Napoleon and Wellington were born—James Watt took out his patent for the steam-engine. Sixteen years later it was applied to the cotton manufacture. In 1785 Boulton and Watt made an engine for a cotton-mill at Papplewick in Notts, and in the same year Ark-wright's patent expired. These two facts taken together mark the introduction of the factory system. But the most famous in-vention of all, and the most fatal to domestic industry, the power-loom, though also patented by Cartwright in 1785, did not come into use for several years,[14] and till the power-loom was introduced the workman was hardly injured. At first, in fact, machinery raised the wages of spinners and weavers owing to the great prosperity it brought to the trade. In fifteen years the cotton trade trebled itself; from 1788 to 1803 has been called its 'golden age'; for, before the power-loom but after the introduc-tion of the mule and other mechanical improvements by which for the first time yarn sufficiently fine for muslin and a variety of other fabrics was spun, the demand became such that 'old barns, cart-houses, out-buildings of all descriptions were repaired, windows broke through the old blank walls, and all fitted up for loom-shops; new weavers' cottages with loom-shops arose in ev-ery direction, every family bringing home weekly from 40 to 120 shillings per week.'[15] At a later date, the condition of the work-man was very different. Meanwhile, the iron industry had been equally revolutionised by the invention of smelting by pit-coal brought into use between 1740 and 1750, and by the application in 1788 of the steam-engine to blast furnaces. In the eight years which followed this later date, the amount of iron manufactured nearly doubled itself.[16]

A further growth of the factory system took place independent of machinery, and owed its origin to the expansion of trade, an expansion which was itself due to the great advance made at this time in the means of communication. The canal system was being rapidly developed throughout the country. In 1777 the Grand Trunk canal, 96 miles in length, connecting the Trent and Mersey, was finished; Hull and Liverpool were connected by one canal while another connected them both with Bristol; and in 1792, the Grand Junction canal, 90 miles in length, made a water-way from London through Oxford to the chief midland towns.[17] Some years afterwards, the roads were greatly improved under Telford and Macadam; between 1818 and 1829 more than a thousand additional miles of turnpike road were constructed;[18] and the next year, 1830, saw the opening of the first railroad. These improved means of communication caused an extraordinary increase in commerce, and to secure a sufficient supply of goods it became the interest of the merchants to collect weavers around them in great numbers, to get looms together in a workshop, and to give out the warp themselves to the workpeople. To these latter this system meant a change from independence to dependence; at the beginning of the century the report of a committee asserts that the essential difference between the domestic and the factory system is, that in the latter the work is done 'by persons who have no property in the goods they manufacture.' Another direct consequence of this expansion of trade was the regular recurrence of periods of over-production and of depression, a phenomenon quite unknown under the old system, and due to this new form of production on a large scale for a distant market.

These altered conditions in the production of wealth necessarily involved an equal revolution in its distribution. In agriculture the prominent fact is an enormous rise in rents. Up to 1795, though they had risen in some places, in others they had been stationary since the Revolution.[19] But between 1790 and

1833, according to Porter, they at least doubled.[20] In Scotland, the rental of land, which in 1795 had amounted to £2,000,000, had risen in 1815 to £5,278,685.[21] A farm in Essex, which before 1793 had been rented at 10s. an acre, was let in 1812 at 50s., though, six years after, this had fallen again to 35s. In Berks and Wilts, farms which in 1790 were let at 14s., were let in 1810 at 70s., and in 1820 at 50s. Much of this rise, doubtless, was due to money invested in improvements—the first Lord Leicester is said to have expended £400,000 on his property[22]—but it was far more largely the effect of the enclosure system, of the consolidation of farms, and of the high price of corn during the French war. Whatever may have been its causes, however, it represented a great social revolution, a change in the balance of political power and in the relative position of classes. The farmers shared in the prosperity of the landlords; for many of them held their farms under beneficial leases, and made large profits by them. In consequence, their character completely changed; they ceased to work and live with their labourers, and became a distinct class. The high prices of the war time thoroughly demoralised them, for their wealth then increased so fast, that they were at a loss what to do with it. Cobbett has described the change in their habits, the new food and furniture, the luxury and drinking, which were the consequences of more money coming into their hands than they knew how to spend.[23] Meanwhile, the effect of all these agrarian changes upon the condition of the labourer was an exactly opposite and most disastrous one. He felt all the burden of high prices, while his wages were steadily falling, and he had lost his common-rights. It is from this period, viz., the beginning of the present century, that the alienation between farmer and labourer may be dated.[24]

Exactly analogous phenomena appeared in the manufacturing world. The new class of great capitalist employers made enormous fortunes, they took little or no part personally in the work of their factories, their hundreds of workmen were individually unknown to them; and as a consequence, the old relations between masters and men disappeared, and a 'cash nexus' was substituted for the human tie. The workmen on their side resorted to combination, and Trades-Unions began a fight which looked as if it were between mortal enemies rather than joint producers.

The misery which came upon large sections of the working people at this epoch was often, though not always, due to a fall in wages, for, as I said above, in some industries they rose. But they suffered likewise from the conditions of labour under the factory system, from the rise of prices, especially from the high price of bread before the repeal of the corn-laws, and from those sudden fluctuations of trade, which, ever since production has been on a large scale, have exposed them to recurrent periods of bitter distress. The effects of the Industrial Revolution prove that free competition may produce wealth without producing well-being. We all know the horrors that ensued in England before it was restrained by legislation and combination.

IX
THE GROWTH
OF PAUPERISM

MALTHUS tells us that his book was suggested by Godwin's *Inquiry*, but it was really prompted by the rapid growth of pauperism which Malthus saw around him, and the book proved the main influence which determined the reform of the English Poor Laws. The problem of pauperism came upon men in its most terrible form between 1795 and 1834. The following statistics will illustrate its growth:

Year	Population	Poor-rate	Per head of Population
1760	7,000,000	£1,250,000	or 3s. 7d.
1784	8,000,000	2,000,000	or 5s. 0d.
1803	9,216,000	4,077,000	or 8s. 11d.
1818	11,876,000	7,870,000	or 13s. 3d.

This was the highest rate ever reached. But really to understand the nature of the problem we must examine the previous history of pauperism, its causes in different periods, and the main influences which determined its increase.

Prejudices have arisen against Political Economy because it seemed to tell men to follow their self-interest and to repress their instincts of benevolence. Individual self-interest makes no provision for the poor, and to do so other motives and ideas must take its place; hence the idea that Political Economy taught that no such provision should be made. Some of the old economists did actually say that people should be allowed to die in the street. Yet Malthus, with all his hatred of the Poor Law, thought that 'the evil was now so deeply seated, and relief given by the Poor Laws so widely extended, that no man of humanity could venture to propose their immediate abolition.'[1] The assumed cruelty of political economy arises from a mistaken conception of its province, and from that confusion of ideas to which

I have before alluded, which turned economic laws into practical precepts, and refused to allow for the action of other motives by their side. What we now see to be required is not the repression of the instincts of benevolence, but their organisation. To make benevolence scientific is the great problem of the present age. Men formerly thought that the simple direct action of the benevolent instincts by means of self-denying gifts was enough to remedy the misery they deplored; now we see that not only thought but historical study is also necessary. Both to understand the nature of pauperism and to discover its effectual remedies, we must investigate its earlier history. But in doing this we should take to heart two warnings: first, not to interpret mediæval statutes by modern ideas; and secondly, not to assume that the causes of pauperism have always been the same.

The history of the Poor Laws divides itself into three epochs; from 1349 to 1601, from 1601 to 1782, and from 1782 to 1834. Now, what was the nature of pauperism in mediæval society, and what were then the means of relieving it? Certain characteristics are permanent in all society, and thus in mediæval life as elsewhere there was a class of impotent poor, who were neither able to support themselves nor had relatives to support them. This was the only form of pauperism in the early beginnings of mediæval society, and it was provided for as follows. The community was then broken up into groups—the manor, the guild, the family, the Church with its hospitals, and each group was responsible for the maintenance of all its members; by these means all classes of poor were relieved. In the towns the craft and religious guilds provided for their own members; large estates in land were given to the guilds, which 'down to the Reformation formed an organised administration of relief' ('the religious guilds were organised for the relief of distress as well as for conjoint and mutual prayer';)[2]—while outside the guilds there were the churches, the hospitals, and the monasteries. The 'settled poor' in towns were relieved by the guilds, in the country by the lords of the manor and the beneficed clergy. 'Every manor had its constitution,'[3] says Professor Stubbs, and, referring to manumission, he adds, 'the native lost the privilege of maintenance which he could claim of his lord.'[4] Among what were called 'the vagrant poor' there were the professional beggars, who were scarcely then considered what we should now call paupers, and 'the valiant labourers' wandering only in search of work. Who then were the paupers? In the towns there were the craftsmen, who could not procure admission into a guild. In the country there was the small class of landless labourers nominally free. It is a great law of social development that the movement from slavery to freedom is also a movement from security to insecurity of maintenance. There is a close connection between the growth of freedom and the growth of pauperism; it is scarcely too much to say that the latter is the price we pay for the former. The first Statute that is in any sense a Poor Law was enacted at a time when the emancipation of the serfs was proceeding rapidly. This is the Statute of Labourers, made in 1349; it has nothing to do with the maintenance of the poor; its object was to repress their vagrancy.[5]

This Statute has been variously interpreted. According to some,[6] it was simply an attempt of the landowners to force the labourers to take the old wages of the times before the Plague. Others object, with Brentano, to this interpretation, and believe that it was not an instance of class legislation, but merely expressed the mediæval idea that prices should be determined by what was thought reasonable and not by competition; for this same Statute regulates the prices of provisions and almost everything which was sold at the time. Probably Brentano is in the main right. It is true that the landowners did legislate with the knowledge that the Statute would be to their own advantage; but the law is none the less in harmony with all the ideas of the age. The Statute affected the labourer in two directions: it fixed his wages, and it prevented him from migrating. It was followed by the Statute of 1388, which is sometimes called the beginning of the English Poor Law. We here find the first distinction between the impotent and the able-bodied poor. This law decreed that if their neighbours would not provide for the poor, they were to seek maintenance elsewhere in the hundred; no one is considered responsible for them; it is assumed that the people of the parish will support them. Here too we catch the first glimpse of a law of settlement in the provision that no labourer or pauper shall wander out of his hundred unless he carry a letter-patent with him.

No exact date can be assigned to the growth of able-bodied pauperism. It was the result of gradual social changes, and of the inability to understand them. Mediæval legislators could not grasp the necessity for the mobility of labour, nor could they see that compulsory provision for the poor was essential, though the Statute of 1388 shows that the bond between lord and dependent was snapped, and security for their maintenance in this way already at an end. The Church and private charity were deemed sufficient; though it is true that laws were passed to prevent the alienation of funds destined for the poor.[7] And with regard to the mobility of labour, we must remember that the vagrancy of the times did not imply the distress of the labourers, but their prosperity. The scarcity of labour allowed of high wages, and the vagrant labourer of the time seems never to have been satisfied, but always wandering in search of still higher wages. The stability of mediæval society depended on the fixity of all its parts, as that of modern society is founded on their mobility. The Statutes afford evidence that high wages and the destruction of old ties did in fact lead to disorder, robbery and violence; and by and by we find the condition of the labourer reversed; in the next period he is a vagrant, because he cannot find work.

In the sixteenth century pauperism was becoming a really serious matter. If we ask, What were its causes then, and what the remedies proposed, we shall find that at the beginning of the century a great agrarian revolution was going on, during which pauperism largely increased. Farms were consolidated, and arable converted into pasture;[8] in consequence, where two hundred men had lived there were now only two or three herdsmen. There was no employment for the dispossessed farmers, who became simple vagabonds, 'valiant beggars,' until later they were absorbed into the towns by the increase of trade. A main cause of the agrarian changes was the dissolution of monasteries, though it was one that acted only indirectly, by the monastic properties passing into the hands of new men who did not hesitate to evict without scruple. About the same time the prices of provisions rose through the influx of the precious metals and the debasement of the coinage. And while the prices of corn in 1541-82 rose 240 per cent. as compared with the past one hundred and forty years, wages rose only 160 per cent.[9] In this fact we discover a second great cause of the pauperism of the time; just as at the end of the eighteenth century we find wages the last to rise, and the labouring man the greatest sufferer from increased prices. As regards the growth of pauperism in towns, the main cause may be found in the confiscation of the estates of the guilds by the Protector Somerset.[10] These guilds had been practically friendly societies, and depended for their funds upon their landed properties.

And how did statesmen then deal with these phenomena? The legislation of the age about 'vagabonds' is written in blood. The only remedy suggested was to punish the vagrant by cruel tortures—by whipping and branding. Even death was resorted to after a second or third offence; and though these penalties proved very ineffectual, the system was not abandoned till the law of 43 Elizabeth recognised that punishment had failed as a remedy. The other class of paupers, the impotent poor, had been directed by a Statute of Richard II. to beg within a certain limited area; in the reigns of Edward VI. and Elizabeth the necessity of compulsory provision for this class of poor slowly dawned upon men's minds. At first the churchwardens were ordered to summon meetings for the purpose of collecting alms, and overseers were appointed who 'shall gently ask and demand' of every man and woman what they of their charity will give weekly towards the relief of the poor. Mayors, head-officers, and churchwardens were to collect money in boxes 'every Sunday and holyday.' The parsons, vicar and curate, were to reason with those who would not give, and if they were not successful, the obstinate person was to be sent to the bishop, who was to 'induce and persuade him'; or by the provisions of a later law, he was to be assessed at Quarter Sessions (1562). Such was the first recognition of the principle of compulsory support, of the fact that there are men in the community whom no one will relieve. There appears upon the scene for the first time the isolated individual, a figure unknown to mediæval society, but who constitutes so striking a phenomenon in the modern world. And hence springs up a new relation between the State and the individual. Since the latter is no longer a member of a compact group, the State itself has to enter into direct connection with him. Thus, by the growth at once of freedom and of poverty, the whole status of the working classes had been changed, and the problem of modern legislation came to be this: to discover how we can have a working class of free men, who shall yet find it easy to obtain sustenance; in other words, how to combine political and material freedom.

All the principles of our modern Poor Laws are found in the next Statute we have to notice, the great law of the 43rd year of Elizabeth, which drew the sharp distinction, ever since preserved, between the able-bodied and the impotent poor. The latter were to be relieved by a compulsory rate collected by the overseers, the former were to be set to work upon materials provided out of the rates; children and orphans were to be apprenticed. From this date 1601, there were no fundamental changes in the law till the end of the eighteenth century. The law of settlement, however, which sprang directly out of the Act of Elizabeth, was added; it was the first attempt to prevent the migration of labourers by other means than punishment. It began with the Statute of 1662, which allowed a pauper to obtain relief only from that parish where he had his settlement, and defined settlement as forty days' residence without interruption; but after this Statute there were constant changes in the law, leading to endless complications; and more litigation took place on this question of settlement than on any other point of the Poor Law. It was not till 1795 that the hardship of former enactments was mitigated by an Act under which no new settler could be removed until he became actually chargeable to the parish.[11]

Two other modifications of the Act of Elizabeth require to be noticed. In 1691 the administration of relief was partially taken out of the hands of the overseers and given to the Justices of the Peace, the alleged reason being that the overseers had abused their power. Henceforth they were not allowed to relieve except by order of a Justice of the Peace, and this provision was construed into a power conferred upon the Justices to give relief independently of any application on the part of the overseers, and led, in fact, to Justices ordering relief at their own discretion. The other important change in the Poor Law was the introduction of the workhouse test in 1722. It is clear that pauperism had grown since the reign of Charles ii. There are many pamphlets of the period full of suggestions as to a remedy, but the only successful idea was this of the workhouse test. Parishes were now empowered to unite and build a workhouse, and refuse relief to all who would not enter it; but the clauses for building workhouses remained inoperative, as very few parishes would adopt them.

The question remains to be asked: Why was pauperism still slowly increasing in the course of the seventeenth and eighteenth centuries in spite of a rise in wages, and, during the first half of the eighteenth century, a low price of corn? Enclosures and the consolidation of farms, though as yet these had been on a comparatively small scale, were partly responsible for it, as they were in an earlier century. Already, in 1727, it was said that some owners were much too eager to evict farmers and cottagers, and were punished by an increase of rates consequent on the evicted tenants sinking into pauperism.[12] By Eden's time the practice of eviction had become general, and the connection between eviction and pauperism is an indisputable fact, though it has been overlooked by most writers. Eden's evidence again shows that pauperism was greatest where enclosures had taken place. At Winslow, for instance, enclosed in 1744 and 1766, 'the rise of the rates was chiefly ascribed to the enclosure of the common fields, which, it was said, had lessened the number of farms, and from the conversion of arable into pasture had much reduced the demand for labourers.' Again, at Kilworth-Beauchamp in Leicestershire, 'the fields being now in pasturage, the farmers had little occasion for labourers, and the poor being thereby thrown out of employment had, of course, to be supported by the parish.'[13] Here too the evil was aggravated by the fate of the ejected farmers, who sank into the condition of labourers, and swelled the numbers of the unemployed. 'Living in a state of servile dependence on the large farmers, and having no prospect to which their hopes could reasonably look forward, their industry was checked, economy was deprived of its greatest stimulation, and their only thought was to enjoy the present moment.' Again, at Blandford, where the same consolidation of farms had been going on, Eden remarks that 'its effects, it is said, oblige small industrious farmers to turn labourers or servants, who, seeing no opening towards advancement, become regardless of futurity, spend their little wages as they receive them without reserving a pension for their old age; and, if incapacitated from working by a sickness which lasts a very short time, inevitably fall upon the parish.'[14]

Besides the enclosure of the common-fields, and the consolidation of farms, the enclosure of the commons and wastes likewise contributed to the growth of pauperism. Arthur Young and Eden thought that commons were a cause of idleness; the labourers wasted their time in gathering sticks or grubbing furze; their pigs and cows involved perpetual disputes with their neighbours, and were a constant temptation to trespass.[15] No doubt this was true where the common was large enough to support the poor without other occupation. But on the other hand, where the labourer was regularly employed, a small common was a great extra resource to him. Arthur Young himself mentions a case at Snettisham in Norfolk, where, when the waste was enclosed, the common rights had been preserved, and as a result of this, combined with the increased labour due to the enclosure, the poor-rates fell from 1s. 6d. to 1s. or 9d., while population grew from five to six hundred. He goes on to say that enclosures had generally been carried out with an utter disregard for the rights of the poor. According to Thornton, the formation of parks contributed to the general result, but I know of no evidence on this head.

A further cause of pauperism, when we come to the end of the century, was the great rise in prices as compared with that in wages. In 1782 the price of corn was 53s. 9¼d., which was considerably higher than the average of the preceding fifty years; but in 1795 it had risen to 81s. 6d., and in the next year it was even more. The corn average from 1795 to 1805 was 81s. 2½d., and from 1805 to 1815 97s. 6d. In 1800 and 1801 it reached the maximum of 127s. and 128s. 6d., which brought us nearer to a famine than we had been since the fourteenth century. Many other articles had risen too. The taxes necessitated by the debt contracted during the American war raised the prices of soap, leather, candles, etc., by one-fifth; butter and cheese rose 1½d. a pound, meat 1d. And meanwhile, 'what advance during the last ten or twelve years,' asks a writer in 1788, 'has been made in the wages of labourers? Very little indeed; in their daily labour nothing at all, either in husbandry or manufactures.' Only by piece-work could they obtain more in nominal wages.[16] Lastly, in the towns there had come the introduction of machinery, the final establishment of the cash-nexus, and the beginning of great fluctuations in trade. In the old days the employer maintained his men when out of work, now he repudiated the responsibility; and the decline in the position of the artisan could be attributed by contemporary writers to 'the iniquitous oppressive practices of those who have the direction of them.'[17]

Such seem to have been the causes of the growth of pauperism and of the degradation of the labourer; the single effective remedy attempted was the workhouse test, and this was abandoned in 1782. But might not landlords and farmers have done something more to check the downward course? Were there no possible remedies? One cannot help thinking the problem might have been solved by common justice in the matter of enclosures. Those who were most in favour of enclosing for the sake of agricultural improvements, like Eden and Young, yet held that, in place of his common field and pasture rights, the labourer should have had an acre, or two acres, or half an acre, as the case might be, attached to his cottage. By such compensation much misery would have been prevented. A more difficult question is, whether anything could have been done directly to relieve the stress of high prices? Burke contended that nothing could be done, that there was no necessary connection between wages and prices; and he would have left the evil to natural remedies.[18] And, as a matter of fact, in the North where there was no artificial interference with wages, the development of mining and manufactures saved the labourer.

In the Midlands and South, where this needful stimulus was absent, the case was different; some increase in the labourer's means of subsistence was absolutely necessary here, in order that he might exist. It would have been dangerous to let things alone, and the true way to meet the difficulty would have been for the farmers to have raised wages—a course of action which they have at times adopted. But an absence alike of intelligence and generosity, and the vicious working of the Poor Laws in the midland and southern counties, prevented this. The farmers refused to recognise the claims alike of humanity and self-interest, so the justices and country gentlemen took the matter into their own hands, while the labourers threw themselves upon the Poor Law and demanded that the parish should do what the farmers refused to do, and should supplement insufficient wages by an allowance. This was the principle which radically vitiated the old Poor Law. The farmers supported the system; they wished every man to have an allowance according to his family, and declared that 'high wages and free labour would overwhelm them.' A change had also come over the minds of the landowners as to their relation to the people. In addition to unthinking and ignorant benevolence, we can trace the growth of a sentiment which admitted an unconditional right on the part of the poor to an indefinite share in the national wealth; but the right was granted in such a way as to keep them in dependence and diminish their self-respect. Though it was increased by the panic of the French revolution, this idea of bribing the people into passiveness was not absolutely new; it had prompted Gilbert's Act in 1782, which abolished the workhouse test, and provided work for those who were willing near their homes. It was this Tory Socialism,[19] this principle of protection of the poor by the rich which gave birth to the frequent use of the term 'labouring poor,' so common in the Statutes and in Adam Smith, an expression which Burke attacked as a detestable canting phrase.[20]

The war with Napoleon gave a new impulse to this pauperising policy. Pitt and the country gentlemen wanted strong armies to fight the French, and reversed the old policy as regards checks upon population. Hitherto they had exercised control over the numbers of the labourers by refusing to build cottages; in 1771, 'an open war against cottages' had been carried on, and landlords often pulled down cottages, says Arthur Young, 'that they may never become the nests, as they are called, of beggar brats.'[21] But now by giving extra allowance to large families, they put a premium on early marriages, and labourers were paid according to the number of their children. Further extension of the allowance system came from actual panic at home. Farmers and landowners were intimidated by the labourers: the landowners had themselves according to Malthus at once inflamed the minds of their labourers and preached to them submission.[22] Rick-burning was frequent; at Swallowfield, in Wiltshire, the justices, 'under the influence of the panic struck by the fires, so far yielded to the importunity of the farmers as to adopt the allowance-system during the winter months.' In 1795 some Berkshire justices 'and other discreet persons' issued a proclamation, which came to be considered as a guide to all the magistrates of the South of England.[23] They declared it to be their unanimous opinion that the state of the poor required further assistance than had been generally given them; and with this view they held it inexpedient to regulate wages according to the statutes of Elizabeth and James; they would earnestly recommend farmers and others to increase the pay of their labourers in proportion to the present price of provisions; but if the farmers refused, they would make an allowance to every poor family in proportion to its numbers. They stated what they thought necessary for a man and his wife and children, which was to be produced 'either by his own and his family's labour on an allowance from the poor-rates.'[24] These were the beginnings of the allowance system, which under its many forms ended in thoroughly demoralising the people; it had not been long in operation before we hear the labourers de scribed as lazy, mutinous, and imperious to the overseers. Whe grants in aid of wages were deemed insufficient, the men woul go to a magistrate to complain, the magistrate would appeal t the humanity of the overseer, the men would add threats, an the overseer would give in. In the parish of Bancliffe 'a man wa employed to look after the paupers, but they threatened t drown him, and he was obliged to withdraw.' The whole charac ter of the people was lowered by the admission that they had right to relief independent of work.

X MALTHUS AND THE LAW OF POPULATION

IT was during this state of things, with population rapidly increasing, that Malthus wrote. Yet he was not thinking directly of the Poor Law, but of Godwin, who, under the influence of Rousseau, had in his *Inquirer* ascribed all human ills to human government and institutions, and drawn bright pictures of what might be in a reformed society. Malthus denied their possibility. Under no system, he contended, could such happiness be insured; human misery was not the result of human injustice and of bad institutions, but of an inexorable law of nature, viz., that population tends to outstrip the means of subsistence. This law would in a few generations counteract the effects of the best institutions that human wisdom could conceive. It is remarkable that though in his first edition he gave a conclusive answer to Godwin, Malthus afterwards made an admission which deducted a good deal from the force of his argument. To the 'positive check' of misery and vice, he added the 'preventive check' of moral restraint, namely, abstinence from marriage.[1] To this Godwin made the obvious reply that such a qualification virtually conceded the perfectibility of society. But Malthus still thought his argument conclusive as against Godwin's Communism.[2] If private property was abolished, he said, all inducements to moral restraint would be taken away. His prophecy has, however, since his time, been refuted by the experience of the communistic societies in America, which proves that the absence of private property is not incompatible with moral restraint.[3]

Is Malthus's law really true? We see that it rests on two premisses. The first is, that the potential rate of increase of the human race is such that population, if unchecked, would double itself in twenty-five years; and Malthus assumes that this rate is constant in every race and at all times. His second premiss is the law of diminishing returns, *i.e.* that after a certain stage of cultivation a given piece of land will, despite any agricultural improvements, yield a less proportionate return to human labour; and this law is true. Malthus did not deny that food might, for a time, increase faster than population; but land could not be increased, and if the area which supplied a people were restricted, the total quantity of food which it produced per head must be at length diminished, though this result might be long deferred. Malthus himself regarded both his conclusions as equally self-evident. 'The first of these propositions,' he says, 'I considered as proved the moment the American increase was related; and the second proposition as soon as it was enunciated.' Why then did he write so long a book? 'The chief object of my work,' he goes on to say, 'was to inquire what effects these laws, which I considered as established in the first six pages, had produced, and were likely to produce, on society;—a subject not very readily exhausted.'[4] The greater part of his essay is an historical examination of the growth of population and the checks on it which have obtained in different ages and countries; and he applies his conclusion to the administration of the Poor Laws in England.

Now there are grave doubts as to the universal truth of his first premiss. Some of his earlier opponents, as Doubleday, laid down the proposition that fecundity varies inversely to nutriment.[5] Thus baldly stated their assertion is not true; but it is an observed fact, as Adam Smith noticed long ago, that the luxurious classes have few children, while a 'half-starved Highland woman' may have a family of twenty.[6] Mr. Herbert Spencer again has asserted that fecundity varies inversely to nervous organisation, and this statement has been accepted by Carey and Bagehot.[7] But it is not so much the increase of brain power as the worry and exhaustion of modern life which tends to bring about this result. Some statistics quoted by Mr. Amasa Walker tend to prove this. He has shown that in Massachusetts, while there are about 980,-000 persons of native birth as against only 260,000 immigrants, the number of births in the two classes is almost exactly the same, the number of marriages double as many in the latter, as in the former, and longevity less and mortality greater among the Americans. Mr. Cliffe-Leslie attributes this fact to a decline in fecundity on the part of American citizens. The whole question, however, is veiled in great obscurity, and is rather for physiologists and biologists to decide; but there do seem to be causes at work which preclude us from assuming with Malthus that the rate of increase is invariable.[8]

Another American writer, Mr. Henry George,[9] has recently argued that Malthus was wrong and Godwin right, that poverty is due to human injustice, to an unequal distribution of wealth, the result of private property in land, and not to Malthus's law of the increase of population or to the law of diminishing returns, both of which he altogether rejects. With regard to the latter he urges with truth that in certain communities, for instance California, where the law of diminishing returns evidently does not come into operation, the same phenomenon of pauperism appears. Now against Mr. George it can be proved by facts that there are cases where his contention is not true. It is noticeable that he makes no reference to France, Norway, and Switzerland—all countries of peasant proprietors, and where consequently the land is not monopolised by a few. But it is certain that in all these countries, at any rate in the present state of agricultural knowledge and skill, the law of diminishing returns does obtain; and it is useless to argue that in these cases it is the injustice of man, and not the niggardliness of nature, that is the cause of poverty, and necessitates baneful checks on population. Still I admit that Mr. George's argument is partially true—a large portion of pauperism and misery is really attributable to bad government and injustice; but this does not touch the main issue, or disprove the law of diminishing returns.

To return to Malthus's first proposition. The phrase that 'population tends to outstrip the means of subsistence' is vague and ambiguous. It may mean that population, if unchecked, *would* outstrip the means of subsistence; or it may mean that population *does* increase faster than the means of subsistence. It is quite clear that, in its second sense, it is not true of England at the present day. The average quantity of food consumed per head is yearly greater; and capital increases more than twice as

fast as population.[10] But the earlier writers on population in-
variably use the phrase in the latter sense, and apply it to the
England of their time. At the present day it can only be true
in this latter sense of a very few countries. It has been said to be
true in the case of India, but even there the assertion can only
apply to certain districts. Mr. George, however, is not content
to refute Malthus's proposition in this sense; he denies it altogether, denies the statement in the sense that population, if unchecked, *would* outstrip the means of subsistence, and lays down
as a general law that there need be no fear of over-population if
wealth were justly distributed. The experience of countries like
Norway and Switzerland, however, where over-population does
exist, although the distribution of wealth is tolerably even, shows
that this doctrine is not universally true. Another criticism of
Mr. George's, however, is certainly good, as far as it goes. Malthus's proposition was supposed to be strengthened by Darwin's
theory, and Darwin himself says that it was the study of Malthus's book which suggested it to him;[11] but Mr. George rightly
objects to the analogy between man and animals and plants. It
is true that animals, in their struggle for existence, have a strictly
limited amount of subsistence, but man can, by his ingenuity
and energy, enormously increase his supply.[12] The objection is
valid, though it can hardly be said to touch the main issue.

I have spoken of the rapid growth of population in the period
we are studying. We have to consider how Malthus accounted
for it, and how far his explanation is satisfactory, as well as what
practical conclusions he came to. In the rural districts he thought
the excessive increase was the consequence of the bad administration of the Poor Laws, and of the premium which they put on
early marriages. This was true, but not the whole truth; there
are other points to be taken into account. In the old days the
younger labourers boarded in the farmhouses, and were of course
single men; no man could marry till there was a cottage vacant,
and it was the policy of the landlords in the 'close villages' to
destroy cottages, in order to lessen the rates.[13] But now the
farmers had risen in social position and refused to board the
labourers in their houses. The ejected labourers, encouraged by

the allowance system, married recklessly,[14] and though some emigrated into the towns, a great evil arose. The rural population kept increasing while the cottage accommodation as steadily diminished, and terrible overcrowding was the result. Owing to the recklessness and demoralisation of the labourer the lack of cottages no longer operated as any check on population.[15] The change in the social habits of the farmers had thus a considerable effect on the increase of rural population and tended to aggravate the effects of the allowance system.

In the towns the greatest stimulus came from the extension of trade due to the introduction of machinery. The artisan's horizon became indistinct; there was no visible limit to subsistence. In a country like Norway, with a stationary society built up of small local units, the labourer knows exactly what openings for employment there are in his community; and it is well known that the Norwegian peasant hesitates about marriage till he is sure of a position which will enable him to support a family.[16] But in a great town, among 'the unavoidable variations of manufacturing labour,'[17] all these definite limits were removed. The artisan could always hope that the growth of industry would afford employment for any number of children—an expectation which the enormously rapid growth of the woollen and cotton manufactures justified to a large extent. And the great demand for children's labour in towns increased a man's income in proportion to the number of his family, just as the allowance system did in the country.[18]

What remedies did Malthus propose? The first was the abolition of the Poor Law; and he was not singular in this opinion. Many eminent writers of the time believed it to be intrinsically bad. He suggested that at a given date it should be announced that no child born after the lapse of a year should be entitled to relief; the improvident were to be left to 'the punishment of nature' and 'the uncertain support of private charity.'[19] Others saw that such treatment would be too hard; that a Poor Law of some sort was necessary, and that the problem was how to secure to the respectable poor the means of support without demoralising them. His second remedy was moral restraint—abstention from marriage till a man had means to support a family, accompanied by perfectly moral conduct during the period of celibacy.[20]

Let us now see what have been the actual remedies. The chief is the reform of the Poor Laws in 1834, perhaps the most beneficent Act of Parliament which has been passed since the Reform Bill. Its principles were (a) the application of the workhouse test and the gradual abolition of outdoor relief to able-bodied labourers; (b) the formation of unions of parishes to promote economy and efficiency, these unions to be governed by Boards of Guardians elected by the ratepayers, thus putting an end to the mischievous reign of the Justices of the Peace; (c) a central Board of Poor Law Commissioners, with very large powers to deal with the Boards of Guardians and control their action; (d) a new bastardy law; (e) a mitigation of the laws of settlement. The effect of the new law was very remarkable. As an example, take the case of Sussex. Before 1834 there were in that county over 6000 able-bodied paupers; two years later there were 124.[21] A similar change took place in almost all the rural districts, and the riots and rick-burning which had been so rife began to grow less frequent. Equally remarkable was the effect upon the rates. In 1818 they were nearly £8,000,000 in England and Wales; in 1837 they had sunk to a little over £4,000,000, and are now only £7,500,000 in spite of the enormous growth of population. The number of paupers, which in 1849 was 930,000, has dwindled in 1881 to 800,000, though the population has meanwhile increased by more than 8,000,000. Notwithstanding this improvement the Poor Laws are by no means perfect, and great reforms are still needed.

Next in importance as an actual remedy we must place emigration. Malthus despised it. He thought that 'from the natural unwillingness of people to desert their native country, and the difficulty of clearing and cultivating fresh soil, it never is or can be adequately adopted'; that, even if effectual for the time, the relief it afforded would only be temporary, 'and the disorders would return with increased virulence.'[22] He could not of course foresee the enormous development which would be given to it by steam navigation, and the close connection established thereby between England and America. Since 1815 eight and a quarter millions of people have emigrated from the United Kingdom; since 1847 three and a half millions have gone from England and Wales alone; and this large emigration has of course materially lightened the labour market. Nor could Malthus any more foresee the great importation of food which would take place in later times. In his day England was insulated by war and the corn laws; now, we import one-half of our food, and pay for it with our manufactures.

As to moral restraint, it is very doubtful, whether it has been largely operative. According to Professor Jevons, writing fifteen years ago, it has been so only to a very small extent.[23] Up to 1860 the number of marriages was rather on the increase; but if among the masses, owing to cheap food, marriages have become more frequent, restraint has on the other hand certainly grown among the middle classes and the best of the artisan class.

I wish to speak of one more remedy, which Malthus himself repudiated,[24] namely, that of artificial checks on the number of children. It has been said that such questions should only be discussed 'under the decent veil of a dead language.' Reticence on them is necessary to wholesomeness of mind; but we ought nevertheless to face the problem, for it is a vital one. These preventive checks on births excite our strong moral repugnance. Men may call such repugnance prejudice, but it is perfectly logical, because it is a protest against the gratification of a strong instinct while the duties attaching to it are avoided. Still our moral repugnance should not prevent our considering the question. Let us examine results. What evidence is there as to the effects of a system of artificial checks? We know that at least one European nation, the French, has to some extent adopted them. Now we find that in the purely rural Department of the Eure, where the population, owing presumably to the widespread adoption of artificial checks, is on the decline, although the district is the best cultivated in France and enjoys considerable material prosperity, the general happiness promised is not found. This Department comes first in statistics of crime; one-third of these crimes are indecent outrages; another third are paltry thefts; and infanticide also is rife.[25] Though this is very incomplete evidence, it shows at least that you may adopt these measures without obtaining the promised results. The idea that a stationary and materially prosperous population will necessarily be free from vice is unreasonable enough in itself, and there is the evidence of experience against it. Indeed, one strong objection to any such system is to be found in the fact that a stationary population is not a healthy condition of things in regard to national life; it means the removal of a great stimulus to progress. One incentive to invention, in particular, is removed in France by attempts to adapt population to the existing means of subsistence; for in this respect it is certainly true that the struggle for existence is essential to progress. Such practices, moreover, prove injurious to the children themselves. The French peasant toils ceaselessly to leave each of his children a comfortable maintenance. It would be better for them to be brought up decently, and then left to struggle for their own maintenance. Much of the genius and inventive power in English towns has come from the rural districts with men belonging to large families, who started in life impressed with the idea that they must win their own way. It is wrong to consider this question from the point of view of wealth alone; we cannot overrate the importance of family life as the source of all that is best in national life. Often the necessity of supporting and educating a large family is a training and refining influence in the lives of the parents, and the one thing that makes the ordinary man conscious of his duties, and turns him into a good citizen. In the last resort we may say that such practices are unnecessary in England at the present day. A man in the superior artisan or middle classes has only to consider *when* he will have sufficient means to rear an average number of children; that is, he need only regulate the time of his marriage. Postponement of marriage, and the willing emigration of some of his children when grown up, does, in his case, meet the difficulty. He need not consider whether there is room in the world for more, for there *is* room; and, in the interests of civilisation, it is not desirable that a nation with a great history and great qualities should not advance in numbers. For the labouring masses, on the other hand, with whom prudential motives have no weight, the only true remedy is to carry out such great measures of social reform as the improvement of their dwellings, better education and better amusements, and thus lift them into the position now held by the artisan, where moral restraints are operative. Above all, it must be remembered that this is not a purely economic problem, nor is it to be solved by mechanical contrivances. To reach the true solution we must tenaciously hold to a high ideal of spiritual life. What the mechanical contrivances might perchance give us is not what we desire for our country. The true remedies, on the other hand, imply a growth towards that purer and higher condition of society for which alone we care to strive.

XI   THE WAGE-FUND THEORY

BESIDES originating the theory of population which bears his name, Malthus was the founder of that doctrine of wages which, under the name of the wage-fund theory, was accepted for fifty years in England. To ascertain what the theory is we may take Mill's statement of it, as given in his review of Thornton *On Labour* in 1869. 'There is supposed to be,' he says, 'at any given instant, a sum of wealth which is unconditionally devoted to the payment of wages of labour. This sum is not regarded as un-alterable, for it is augmented by saving, and increases with the progress of wealth; but it is reasoned upon as at any given mo-ment a predetermined amount. More than that amount it is as-sumed that the wages-receiving class cannot possibly divide among them; that amount, and no less, they cannot possibly fail to obtain. So that the sum to be divided being fixed, the wages of each depend solely on the divisor, the number of partici-pants.'[1] This theory was implicitly believed from Malthus's time to about 1870; we see it accepted, for instance, in Miss Marti-neau's Tales. And from the theory several conclusions were de-duced which, owing to their practical importance, it is well to put in the forefront of our inquiry as to its truth. It is these conclusions which have made the theory itself and the science to which it belongs an offence to the whole working class. It was said in the first place that according to the wage-fund theory, Trades-Unions could not at any given time effect a general rise in wages. It was, indeed, sometimes admitted that in a particular trade the workmen could obtain a rise by combination, but this could only be, it was alleged, at the expense of workmen in other trades. If, for instance, the men in the building trade got higher wages through their Union, those in the iron foundries or in some other industry must suffer to an equivalent extent. In the next place it was argued that combinations of workmen could not in the long-run increase the fund out of which wages were paid. Capital might be increased by saving, and, if this saving was more rapid than the increase in the number of labourers, wages would rise, but it was denied that Unions could have any effect in forcing such an increase of saving. And hence it followed that the only real remedy for low wages was a limitation of the number of the labourers. The rate of wages, it was said, depended entirely on the efficacy of checks to population.

The error lay in the premisses. The old economists, it may be observed, very seldom examined their premisses. For this theory assumes— (1) that either the capital of a particular individual available for the payment of wages is fixed, or, at any rate, the total capital of the community so available is fixed; and (2) that wages are always paid out of capital. Now it is plainly not true that a particular employer makes up his mind to spend a fixed quantity of money on labour;[2] the amount spent varies with a number of circumstances affecting the prospect of profit on the part of the capitalist, such, for instance, as the price of labour. Take the instance of a strike of agricultural labourers in Ireland, given by Mr. Trench to Nassau Senior. He was employing one hundred men at 10d. a day, thus spending on wages £25 a week. The men struck for higher pay—a minimum of 1s. 2d., and the more capable men to have more. Trench offered to give the wages asked for, but greatly reduced his total expenditure, as it would not pay to employ so many men at the higher rate. Thus only seventeen were employed; the other eighty-three objected, and it ended in all going back to work at the old rate.[3] The fact is, that no individual has a fixed wage-fund, which it is not in his power either to diminish or increase. Just as he may reduce the total amount which he spends on labour, rather than pay a rate of wages which seems incompatible with an adequate profit, so he may increase that total amount, in order to augment the wages of his labourers, by diminishing the sum he spends upon himself or by employing capital which is lying idle, if he thinks that even with the higher rate of wages he can secure a sufficiently remunerative return upon his investment. Thus the workman may, according to circumstances, get higher or lower wages than the current rate, without any alteration in the quantity of employment given. When wages in Dorset and Wilts were 7s.,[4] the labourers, if they had had sufficient intelligence and power of combination, might have forced the farmers to pay them 8s. or 9s., for the latter were making very high profits. As a matter of fact, where the workmen have been strong, and the profits made by the employers large, the former have often forced the employers to give higher wages.

Neither is it true that there is in the hands of the community as a whole, at any given time, a fixed quantity of capital for supplying the wants of the labourers, so much food, boots, hats, clothes, etc., which neither employers nor workmen can increase. It used to be said that a rise in money wages would simply mean that the price of all the commodities purchased by the labourers would rise proportionately, owing to the increase of demand, and that their real wages, *i.e.* the number of things they could purchase with their money, would be no greater than before. But, as a matter of fact, the supply can be increased as fast as the demand. It is true that between two harvests the available quantity of corn is fixed, but that of most other commodities can be increased at a short notice. For commodities are not stored up for consumption in great masses, but are being continually produced as the demand for them arises.

So far I have been speaking of the theory as applied to wages at a particular time. Now, what did it further imply of wages in the long-run? According to Ricardo's law, which has been adopted by Lassalle and the Socialists, wages depend on the ratio between population and capital. Capital may be *gradually* increased by saving, and population *may* be gradually diminished; but Ricardo thought that the condition of the labourer was surely on the decline, because population was advancing faster than capital. While admitting occasionally that there had been changes in the standard of comfort, he yet disregarded these in his general theory, and assumed that the standard was fixed; that an increase of wages would lead to an increase of population, and that wages would thus fall again to their old rate, or even lower. The amount of corn consumed by the labourer would not diminish, but that of all other commodities would decline.[5] Later economists have qualified this statement of the supposed law. Mill showed that the standard of comfort was not fixed, but might vary indefinitely. This being the case, the labourer might sink even lower than Ricardo supposed possible, for population might increase till the labourer had not only less of everything else, but was forced down to a lower staple of life than corn, for instance, potatoes. And this has, as a matter of fact, taken place in some countries. But, on the other hand, the standard might rise, as it has risen in England; and Mill thought that it would rise yet more. At first this was his only hope for the working classes.[6] At a later period he trusted that the labourer, by means of co-operation, might become more and more self-employing, and so obtain both profits and wages.

It is interesting to inquire how this wage-fund theory grew up. Why was it held that employers could not give higher real wages? Its origin is easy to understand. When Malthus wrote his essay on population, there had been a series of bad harvests, and in those days but small supplies of corn could be obtained from abroad. Thus year after year there seemed to be a fixed quantity of food in the country and increasing numbers requiring food. Population was growing faster than subsistence, and increased money wages could not increase the quantity of food that was to be had. Thus in 1800, when corn was 127s. the quarter, it was clear that the rich could not help the poor by giving them higher wages, for this would simply have raised the price of the fixed quantity of corn. Malthus assumed that the amount of food was practically fixed; therefore, unless population diminished, as years went on, wages would fall, because worse soils would be cultivated and there would be increased difficulty in obtaining food.[7] But the period he had before his eyes was quite exceptional; after the peace, good harvests came and plenty of corn; food grew cheaper, though population advanced at the same rate. So that the theory in this shape was true only of the twenty years from 1795 to 1815. But, when it had once been said that wages depended on the proportion between population and food, it was easy to substitute capital for food and say that they depended on the proportion between population and capital, food and capital being wrongly identified.[8] Then when the identification was forgotten, it was supposed that there is at any given moment a fixed quantity of wage-capital—food, boots, hats, furniture, clothes, etc.—destined for the payment of wages, which neither employers nor workmen can diminish or increase, and thus the rate of wages came to be regarded as regulated by a natural law, independent of the will of either party.[9]

We have already seen that this theory is false; we have now to substitute for it some truer theory, and explain thereby the actual phenomena of the labour market, such, for instance, as the fact that wages at Chicago or New York are twice as high as they are in England, while the prices of the necessaries of life are lower. Though modern economists have pointed out the fallacies of the old wage-fund theory, no economist has yet succeeded in giving us a complete theory of wages in its place. I believe indeed that so complicated a set of conditions as are involved cannot be explained by any one formula, and that the attempt to do so leads to fallacies. Yet I am also aware that the public seem to feel themselves aggrieved that economists will not now provide them with another convenient set phrase in place of the wage-fund theory, and are inclined to doubt the validity of their explanations in consequence. Now, wages in a given country depend on two things: the total amount of produce in the country, and the manner in which that produce is divided. To work out the former problem we must investigate all the causes which affect the whole amount of wealth produced, the natural resources of the country, its political institutions, the skill, intelligence, and inventive genius of its inhabitants. The division of the produce, on the other hand, is determined mainly by the proportion between the number of labourers seeking employment and the quantity of capital seeking investment; or, to put the case in a somewhat different way, instead of saying that wages are paid out of stored-up capital, we now say that they are the labourer's share of the produce.[10] What the labourer's share will be depends first on the quantity of produce he can turn out, and

secondly, on the nature of the bargain which he is able to make
with his employer. We are now in a position to explain the question put above, why wages in America are double what they are
in England. An American ironmaster, if asked to give a reason
for the high wages he pays, would say that the land determines
the rate of wages in America, because under the Free Homestead
Law, any man can get a piece of land for a nominal sum, and no
puddler will work for less than he can get by working on this
land.[11] Now, in the Western States the soil is very fertile, and
though the average yield is lower than in Wiltshire, the return
in proportion to the labour expended is greater. Moreover, labour being scarce, the workman has to be humoured; he is in
a favourable position in making his bargain with the employer,
and obtains a large share of the produce. Thus agricultural
wages are very high, and this explains also the cause of high
wages in the American iron-trade and other American industries.
In consequence of these high wages the manufacturer is obliged
to make large use of machinery, and much of our English machinery, *e.g.* that of the Leicester boot and shoe trade, has been
invented in America. Now, better machinery makes labour more
efficient and the produce per head of the labourers greater. Further, according to the testimony of capitalists, the workmen work
harder in America than in England, because they work with
hope; they have before them the prospect of rising in the world
by their accumulations. Thus it is that the produce of American
manufactures is great, and allows of the labourer obtaining a
large share. High wages in America are therefore explained by
the quantity of produce the labourer turns out being great and
by the action of competition being in his favour.

There are, however, other causes influencing the rate of wages
in America which are less favourable to the workmen. Protection, for instance, diminishes real wages by enhancing the cost of
many articles in common use, such as cutlery. It is owing to
Protection also that capitalists are able to obtain exceptionally
high profits at the expense of the workmen. By combining and
forming rings they can govern the market, and not only control
prices but dictate the rate of wages. Six or seven years ago, the

whole output of Pennsylvanian anthracite was in the hands of a
few companies. Hence it was that, in the Labour War of 1877,
the workmen declared that, while they did not mind wages being
fixed by competition, they would not endure their being fixed by
rings, and that such rings would produce a revolution. And the
monopoly of these companies was only broken through by a great
migration of workmen to the West. The experience of America
in this instance is of interest in showing how, as industry advances, trade tends to get concentrated into fewer hands; hence
the danger of monopolies. It has even been asserted that Free
Trade must lead to great natural monopolies. This may be true
of a country like America which has internal but not external
free trade, but only of such a country; for foreign competition
would prevent a knot of capitalists from ever obtaining full control of the market.

I have shown why wages are higher in America than in England. We may go on to inquire why they are higher in England
than in any other part of Europe. The great reason is that the
total amount of wealth produced in this country is larger, and
that from a variety of causes, material and moral. The chief
material causes are our unrivalled stores of coal and iron, and
perhaps, above all, our geographical position. On the moral
side, our political institutions, being favourable to liberty, have
developed individual energy and industry in a degree unknown
in any other country. On the other hand, it has been said that
the exclusion of the labourer from the land in England must
have tended to lower wages. And no doubt the adoption of a
system of large farms has driven the labourers into the towns,
and made the competition for employment there very keen. But,
to set against this, the efficiency of English manufacturing labour
is largely due to this very fact, that it is not able to shift on to
the land. While in America the whole staff of a cotton factory
may be changed in three years, in England the artisan 'sticks to
his trade,' and brings up his children to it; and thus castes are
formed with inherited aptitudes, which render labour more efficient, and its produce greater. I believe the higher wages obtained in England, in comparison with the Continent, are mainly

due to greater efficiency of labour—that this is the chief cause
why the total produce is greater. But if we go further, and ask
what determines the division of the produce, the answer must be:
mainly competition. To return to the comparison with America,
the reason why the English labourer gets lower wages than the
American is the great competition for employment in the over-
stocked labour-market of this country.

I must notice an objection to the theory of wages as stated
above. Wages, I have explained, are the labourers' share of the
produce, and are paid out of it. But, it may be said, while our
new Law Courts, or an ironclad, are being built—operations
which take a long time before there is any completed result—
how can it be correctly held that the labourer is paid out of the
produce? It is of course perfectly true that he is maintained during such labours only by the produce of others; and that unless
some great capitalist had either accumulated capital, or borrowed it, the labourer could not be paid. But this has nothing
to do with the rate of wages. That is determined by the amount
of the produce and is independent of the method of payment.
What the capitalist does is merely to pay in advance the labourer's share, as a matter of convenience.

We will next inquire what are the limits to a rise of wages in
any particular trade? The answer depends on two things. First,
Is the capitalist getting more than the ordinary rate of profits?
If he is not, he will resist a rise on the ground that he 'cannot
afford' to pay more wages. This is what an arbitrator, for instance, might say if he examined the books, and he would mean
by it that, if the employer had to raise his wages, he would have
to be content with lower profits than he could make in other
trades. As a matter of fact, however, capitalists often do make
exceptionally high profits, and it is in such cases that Trades-
Unions have been very successful in forcing them to share these
exceptional profits with their men. Secondly, though the employer be getting only ordinary profits, his workmen may still be
strong enough to force him to give higher wages, but he will
only do so permanently if he can compensate himself by raising
the price of his commodity. Thus the second limit to a rise in

wages in a particular trade is the amount which the consumer can be forced to pay for its products. Workmen have often made mistakes by not taking this into account, and have checked the demand for the articles which they produced, and so brought about a loss both to their masters and themselves.[12] In a particular trade then the limit to a rise in wages is reached when any further rise will drive the employer out of the trade, or when the increased price of the commodity will check the demand. When dealing with the general trade of a country, however, we can neglect prices altogether, since there can be no such thing as a general rise in prices while the value of the precious metal is stationary. Could, then, the whole body of the workmen throughout the kingdom, by good organisation, compel employers to accept lower profits? If there was a general strike, would it be the interest of the employers to give way? It is impossible to answer such a question beforehand. It would be a sheer trial of strength between the two parties, the outcome of which cannot be predicted, for nothing of the kind has ever actually taken place. And though there is now a nearer approximation than ever before to the supposed conditions, there has as yet been nothing like a general organisation of workmen.

Assuming, however, that the workmen succeeded in such a strike, we can then ask what would be the effect of a general rise of wages in the long-run? One of several results might ensue. The remuneration of employers having declined, their numbers might diminish, and the demand for labour would then diminish also and wages fall. Or again the decline in the rate of interest might check the accumulation of capital, thus again diminishing the demand for labour. Or, on the other hand, the rise in wages might be permanent, the remuneration of employers still proving sufficient, and the accumulation of capital remaining unchecked. Or lastly, higher wages might lead to greater efficiency of labour, and in this case profits would not fall. It is impossible to decide on *a priori* grounds which of these results would actually take place.

Returning to our period, we may apply these principles to explain the fall in wages between 1790 and 1820. During this period, while rent was doubled, interest also was nearly doubled (this by the way disproves Mr. George's theory on that point),[13] and yet wages fell. We may take Mr. Porter's estimate. 'In some few cases there had been an advance of wages, but this occurred only to skilled artisans, and even with them the rise was wholly incommensurate with the increased cost of all the necessaries of life. The mere labourer . . . did not participate in this partial compensation for high prices, but was . . . at the same or nearly the same wages as had been given before the war.' In 1790 the weekly wage skilled artisans and farm labourers respectively would buy 82 and 169 pints of corn: in 1800 they would buy 53 and 83.[14] According to Mr. Barton, a contemporary writer, wages between 1760 and 1820, 'estimated in money, had risen 100 per cent.; estimated in commodities, they had fallen 33 per cent.'[15] What were the causes of this fall? Let us first take the case of the artisans and manufacturing labourers. One cause in their case was a series of bad harvests. To explain how this would affect wages in manufactures we must fall back on the deductive method, and assume certain conditions from which to draw our conclusions. Let us suppose two villages side by side, one agricultural, the other manufacturing, in the former of which the land is owned by landowners, and tilled by labour employed by farmers. Suppose the manufacturing village to be fed by its neighbours in exchange for cutlery. Then, if there is a bad harvest in the agricultural village, every labourer in the manufacturing village will have to spend more on corn. The owners of land will gain enormously; the farmers will be enriched in so far as they can retain the increased prices for themselves, which they will do, if holding on leases. But every one else will be poorer, for there has been a loss of wealth. In order to get his corn, the labourer will have to give more of his share of the produce; and hence the demand for all other goods, which are produced for the labourers' consumption, will diminish. Nothing affects the labourer so much as good or bad harvests, and it is because of its tendency to neutralise the consequences of deficient crops at home, that the labourer has gained so much by Free Trade. When we have a bad harvest here, we get plenty of corn from America, and the labourer pays nearly the same price for his loaf, and has as much money as before left to spend on other commodities. Still, even at the present day, some depression of trade is generally associated with bad harvests. And though Free Trade lessens the force of their incidence on a particular locality, it widens the area affected by them—a bad harvest in Brazil may prejudice trade in England.

The next point to be taken into consideration is the huge taxation which fell upon the workmen at this time; even as late as 1834 half the labourers' wages went in taxes. There was also increase in the National Debt. During the war we had nominally borrowed £600,000,000, although owing to the way in which the loans were raised, the actual sum which came into the national exchequer was only £350,000,000. All this capital was withdrawn from productive industry, and the demand for labour was diminished to that extent. Lastly, the labourer was often actually paid in bad coin, quantities of which were bought by the manufacturers for the purpose; and he was robbed by the truck system, through which the employer became a retail trader, with power to over-price his goods to an indefinite extent.

Some of these causes affected the agricultural and manufacturing labourers alike; they suffered, of course, equally from bad harvests. But we have seen in former lectures that there were agrarian and social changes during this period, which told upon the agricultural labourer exclusively. The enclosures took away his common-rights, and where the land, before enclosure, had been already in cultivation, they diminished the demand for his labour, besides depriving him of the hope of becoming himself a farmer, and, to mention a seemingly small but really serious loss, cutting off his supply of milk, which had been provided by the 'little people' who kept cows on the commons. He was further affected by the enormous rise in cottage rents. Mr. Drummond, a Surrey magistrate, told the Commission on Labourers' Wages in 1824, that he remembered cottages with good gardens letting for 30s. before the war, while at the time when he was speaking the same were fetching £5, £7, or £10.

This rise was due to causes we have before had in review, to the growth of population, the expulsion of servants from the farmhouses, and the demolition of cottages in close villages. When the labourers, to meet the deficiency, built cottages for themselves on the wastes, the farmers pulled them down, and, if the labourers rebuilt them, refused to employ them, with the result that such labourers became thieves and poachers.[16] Again, during this period, it was not uncommon for the farmers absolutely to determine what wages should be paid, and the men in their ignorance were entirely dependent on them. Here are two facts to prove their subservience. In one instance, two pauper families who had cost their parish no less than £20 a year each, were given instead an acre of land rent free, and the rates were relieved to that amount; but though successful, the experiment was discontinued, 'lest the labourer should become independent of the farmer.'[17] And this is the statement of an Essex farmer in 1793: 'I was the more desirous to give them an increase of pay, as it was unasked for by the men, who were content with less than they had a right to expect.' The agricultural labourer at this time was in an entirely helpless condition in bargaining with his employer. Nor were the farmers the only class who profited by his deterioration; for the high rents of the time were often paid out of the pocket of the labourer. The period was one of costly wars, bad seasons, and industrial changes. The misfortunes of the labouring classes were partly inevitable, but they were also largely the result of human injustice, of the selfish and grasping use made of a power which exceptional circumstances had placed in the hands of landowners, farmers, and capitalists.

XII

RICARDO AND THE GROWTH OF RENT

In Political Economy, as in other sciences, a careful study of method is an absolute necessity. And this subject of method will come into special prominence in the present lecture, because we have now to consider the writings of a man of extraordinary intellect and force, who, beyond any other thinker, has left the impress of his mind on economic method. Yet even he would have been saved from several fallacies, if he had paid more careful attention to the necessary limitations of the method which he employed. It may be truly said that David Ricardo has produced a greater effect even than Adam Smith on the actual practice of men as well as on the theoretical consideration of social problems. His book has been at once the great prop of the middle classes, and their most terrible menace; the latter, because from it have directly sprung two great text-books of Socialism, *Das Kapital* of Karl Marx, and the *Progress and Poverty* of Mr. Henry George. And yet for thirty or forty years Ricardo's writings did more than those of any other author to justify in the eyes of men the existing state of society.

Ricardo's life has little in it of external interest. He made his fortune on the Stock Exchange by means of his great financial abilities, and then retired and devoted himself to literature. During the few years that he sat in Parliament, he worked (we have it on Huskisson's testimony) a great change in the opinions of legislators, even in those of the country squires—a remarkable fact, since his speeches are highly abstract, and contain few allusions to current politics, reading in fact like chapters from his book. We may notice one direct effect of his speeches: they were the most powerful influence in determining the resumption of cash payments. In his private life he associated much with Bentham and James Mill.

James Mill, like Bentham and Austin, was a staunch adherent
of the deductive method, and it was partly through Mill's influence that Ricardo adopted it. Mill was his greatest friend; it was
he who persuaded him both to go into Parliament, and to pub-
lish his great book. Ricardo's political opinions in fact merely
reflect those of James Mill, and the other philosophical Radicals
of the time, though in Political Economy he was their teacher.
Ricardo reigned without dispute in English Economics from
1817 to 1848, and though his supremacy has since then been
often challenged, it is by no means entirely overthrown. His
influence was such that his method became the accepted method
of economists; and to understand how great the influence of
method may be, you should turn from his writings and those of
his followers to Adam Smith, or to Sir Henry Maine, where you
come in contact with another cast of mind, and will find your-
selves in a completely different mental atmosphere. Now what is
this deductive method which Ricardo employed? It consists in
reasoning from one or two extremely simple propositions down
to a series of new laws. He always employed this method, taking
as his great postulate that all men will on all matters follow
their own interests. The defect of the assumption lies in its
too great simplicity as a theory of human nature. Men do not
always know their own interest. Bagehot points out that the £10
householders, who were enfranchised by the first Reform Bill,
were after 1832 the most heavily taxed class in the community,
though the remedy was in their own hands; because they were
ignorant and apathetic. And even when men know their interests, they will not always follow them; other influences intervene, custom, prejudice, even fear. Cairnes frankly admits these
defects in Ricardo's method;[1] but it took economists some thirty
or forty years to learn the necessity of testing their conclusions
by facts and observations.[2] Since 1848 their attitude has improved; it is now seen that we must insist upon the verification
of our premisses, and examine our deductions by the light of
history.

Ricardo has deduced from very simple data a famous law of
industrial progress. In an advancing community, he says, rent

must rise, profits fall, and wages remain about the same.[3] We shall find from actual facts that this law has been often true, and is capable of legitimate application, though Mr. Cliffe-Leslie would repudiate it altogether; but it cannot be accepted as a universal law. The historical method, on the other hand, is impotent of itself to give us a law of progress, because so many of the facts on which it relies are, in Economics, concealed from us. By the historical method we mean the actual observation of the course of economic history, and the deduction from it of laws of economic progress; and this method, while most useful in checking the results of deduction is, by itself, full of danger from its tendency to set up imperfect generalisations. Sir H. Maine and M. Laveleye, for instance, have taken an historical survey of land-tenure, and drawn from it the conclusion that the movement of property in land is always from collective to individual ownership; and Mr. Ingram,[4] again, alluding to this law, accepts it as true that there is a natural tendency towards private property in land. He can build his argument on the universal practice from Java to the Shetlands, and it would seem a legitimate conclusion that the tendency will be constant. Yet there is at the present day a distinct movement towards replacing private by collective ownership, due to the gradual change in the opinions of men as to the basis on which property in land should rest. Mill, in 1848, argued that where the cultivator was not also the owner, there was no justification for private ownership; later in his life, he advocated the confiscation of the unearned increment in land.[5] If we ask, 'Was he right?' the answer must be: Every single institution of society is brought to the test of utility and general national well-being; hence, private property in land, if it fails under this test, will not continue. So too with the rate of interest: older economists have insisted on the necessity of a certain rate, in order to encourage the accumulation of capital; but we may fairly ask whether the rate of remuneration for the use of capital is not too high—whether we could not obtain sufficient capital on easier terms? These considerations show that, in predicting the actual course of industrial progress, we must not be content to say that because there has been a movement in a certain direction in the past—for example, one from status to contract—it will therefore continue in the future. We must always apply the test, Does it fit in with the urgent present requirements of human nature?

Ricardo's influence on legislation, to which I have already alluded, was twofold; it bore directly upon the special subject of currency and finance; and, what is more remarkable, it affected legislation in general. As regards finance, his pamphlets are the real justification of our monetary system, and are still read by all who would master the principles of currency. With respect to other legislation, he and his friends have the great credit of having helped to remove not merely restrictions on trade in general, but those in particular which bore hardest on the labourer. When Joseph Hume, in 1824, proposed the repeal of the Combination Laws, he said he had been moved thereto by Ricardo. But though Ricardo advocated the removal of restrictions which injured the labourer, he deprecated all restrictions in his favour; he ridiculed the Truck Acts, and supported the opposition of the manufacturers to the Factory Acts—an opposition which, be it remembered, though prompted by mere class interest, was also supported in the name and on the then accepted principles of economic science.

In this way Ricardo became the prop, as I have called him, of the middle classes. Throughout his treatise there ran the idea of natural law, which seemed to carry with it a sort of justification of the existing constitution of society as inevitable. Hence his doctrines have proved the readiest weapons wherewith to combat legislative interference or any proposals to modify existing institutions. Hence, too, his actual conclusions, although gloomy and depressing, were accepted without question by most of his contemporaries. Another school, however, has grown up, accepting his conclusions as true under existing social conditions, but seeing through the fallacy of his 'natural law.' These are the Socialists, through whom Ricardo has become a terror to the middle classes. The Socialists believe that, by altering the social conditions which he assumed to be unalterable, Ricardo's conclusions can be escaped. Karl Marx and Lassalle have adopted

Ricardo's law of wages; but they have argued that, since by this law wages, under our present social institutions, can never be more than sufficient for the bare subsistence of the labourer, we are bound to reconsider the whole foundation of society. Marx also simply accepts Ricardo's theory of value. The value of products, said Ricardo, is determined by the quantity of the labour expended on them; and Marx uses this statement to deduce the theorem that the whole value of the produce rightly belongs to labour, and that by having to share the produce with capital the labourer is robbed.

Mr. Henry George, again, the latest Socialist writer, is purely and entirely a disciple of Ricardo. The whole aim of his treatise, *Progress and Poverty*, is to prove that rent must rise as society advances and wealth increases.[6] It is not the labourer, Ricardo reasoned, who will be the richer for this progress, nor the capitalist, but the owner of land. Mr. George's theory of progress is the same. Putting aside his attempt to show a connection between the laws of interest and wages, which he contends will rise and fall together, there is little difference between his conclusions and Ricardo's. Others before Mr. George had clearly enough seen this bearing of the law of rent. Roesler, the German economist, says: 'Political Economy would only be a theory of human degradation and impoverishment, if the law of rent worked without modification.'[7]

Now let us see what are the assumptions on which Ricardo grounded his law about the course of rent, wages, and profits in a progressive community. The pressure of population, he argued, makes men resort to inferior soils; hence the cost of agricultural produce increases, and therefore rent rises. But why will profits fall? Because they depend upon the cost of labour,[8] and the main element in determining this is the cost of the commodities consumed by the workmen. Ricardo assumes that the standard of comfort is fixed. If, therefore, the cost of a quartern loaf increases, and the labourer is to obtain the same number of them, his wages must rise, and profits therefore must fall. Lastly, why should wages remain stationary? Because, assuming that the labourer's standard of comfort is fixed, a rise of wages or a fall in prices will only lead to a proportionate increase of population. The history of the theory of rent is very interesting, but it is out of our road, so I can only lightly touch upon it. Adam Smith had no clear or consistent theory at all on the subject, and no distinct views as to the relation between rent and price. The modern doctrine is first found in a pamphlet by a practical farmer named James Anderson, published in 1777, the year after the appearance of *The Wealth of Nations;* [9] but it attracted little attention till it was simultaneously re-stated by Sir Edward West, and by Malthus in his pamphlet on the Corn Laws. [10] Had the theory, however, been left in the shape in which they stated it, it would have had little influence. It was Ricardo, who, puzzled by the question of rent, snatched at the theory, and gave it currency by embodying it in his whole doctrine of value and of economic development.

Ricardo's two great positive conclusions are: first, that the main cause of rent is the necessity of cultivating inferior soil as civilisation advances; and secondly, that rent is not the cause but the result of price. [11] The theory has been disputed and criticised, but nearly all the objections have come from persons who have not understood it. We may say conclusively that, as a theory of the causes of rent, apart from that general doctrine of industrial development of which in Ricardo it forms a part, the theory is true. The one formidable objection which can be urged against it is that the rise in rents in modern times has been due not so much to the necessity of resorting to inferior soils, as to improvements in agriculture; but when Professor Thorold Rogers[12] attacks the theory on this ground, he merely proves that Ricardo has overlooked some important causes which have led to an increase of rents since the Middle Ages.

What, then, are we justified in stating to be the ultimate causes of rent? First, the fertility of the soil and the skill of the cultivator, by which he is able to raise a larger produce than is necessary for his own subsistence; this makes rent physically possible. Next, the fact that land is limited in quantity and quality; that is, that the supply of the land most desirable from its situation and fertility is less than the demand: this allows of rent being exacted.[13] The early colonists in America paid no rent, because there was an abundance of land open to every one; but twenty years later, rent was paid because population had grown. Let us see exactly what happens in such a case. A town is founded on the sea-coast; as it grows, the people in that town have to get some of their food from a distance. Assume that the cost of raising that corn and bringing it to the town is 20s., and that the cost of raising it close to the town is 15s. for every five bushels (we will suppose that in the latter instance the cost of carriage is *nil*); then, as both quantities will be sold at the same price, the surplus 5s. in the latter case will go for rent. Thus we find that rent has arisen because corn is brought into the market at different costs. In twenty years more, rents will have risen still further, because soils still more inferior in fertility or situation will have been brought into cultivation. But the rise of rent is not directly due to the cultivation of inferior soils; the direct cause is the increase of population which has made that cultivation necessary.

Going back to the question raised by Professor Rogers, as to the effect of agricultural improvements on rent, we may notice that the controversy on this question was first fought out between Ricardo and Malthus. Ricardo thought that improvements would lead to a fall in rents; Malthus maintained the opposite, and he was right. Take an acre of land close to the town, such as we were considering above, with an original produce of five bushels of wheat, but which, under improved cultivation, yields forty bushels. If the price of wheat remains the same, and all the land under cultivation has been improved to an equivalent extent, the rent will now be 5s. multiplied by eight. Yet there are a few historical instances where agricultural improvements have been followed by a fall in rents. For instance, during the Thirty Years' War the Swiss supplied Western Germany with corn, and introduced improvements into their agriculture, in order to meet the pressure of the demand. After the peace of Westphalia the demand fell off; the Swiss found they were producing more than they could sell; prices fell, and, as a consequence, rents fell also.[14]

Professor Rogers has further objected to Ricardo's theory that it does not explain the historical origin of rent. The term 'rent' is ambiguous; it has been used for the payment of knight-service, for the performances of religious offices, for serfs' labour and the sum of money for which it was commuted. In Ricardo's mouth it meant only the money rent paid by a capitalist farmer, expecting the usual rates of profits; but it is quite true that these modern competition rents did not arise till about the time of James I.[15]

The last point in the theory of rent is the relation between rent and price. Before Ricardo's time most practical men thought that rent was a cause of price. Ricardo answered, There is land cultivated in England which pays no rent, or at least there is capital employed in agriculture which pays none; therefore there is in the market corn which has paid no rent, and it is the cost of raising this corn, which is grown on the poorest land, that determines the price of all the corn in the same market.[16] Probably he was right in his statement that there is land in England which pays no rent; but even if all land and all farmers' capital paid rent, it would not affect the argument, which says that rent is not the cause but the result of price. We may conclude that at the present day rent is determined by two things: the demand of the population, and the quantity and quality of land available. These determine it by fixing the price of corn.

Now let us turn to facts, to see how our theories work. We will take the rise in rents between 1790 and 1830, and ask how it came about. The main causes were— (1) Improvements in agriculture, the chief of which were the destruction of the common-field system, rendering possible the rotation of crops, the consolidation of farms with the farmhouse in the centre of the holding, and the introduction of machinery and manures; (2) the great growth of population, stimulated by mechanical inventions; (3) a series of bad harvests, which raised the price of corn to an unparalleled height; (4) the limitation of supply, the population having to be fed with the produce of England itself, since, during the first part of the period all supplies from abroad were cut off by war, and later, higher and higher protective du-

ties were imposed, culminating in the famous corn bill of 1815
After 1815, however, a fall in rents—not a very great one—took
place, a process which greatly puzzled people at the time. It was
the consequence of a sudden coincidence of agricultural improvements and good harvests; there was for a time an over production of corn, and wheat fell in price from 90s. to 35s. This
fact is the explanation of Ricardo's mistaken idea that agricultural improvements tend to reduce rents. Having no historical turn of mind, such as Malthus had, he did not recognise
that this effect of agricultural improvements was quite accidental. This case, indeed, and the instance of Switzerland given
above, with the similar events in Germany about 1820, are the
only historical examples of such an effect. For a time there was
great agricultural distress; the farmers could not get their rents
reduced in proportion to the fall in prices, and many, in spite of
the enormous profits they had before made under beneficial
leases, were ruined; the farming class never wholly recovered till
the repeal of the Corn Laws. But the fall was temporary and
exceptional. Taking the period as a whole its striking feature is
the rise of rents, and this rise was due to the causes stated: increased demand on the part of an increased population, and
limitation of quantity, with improved quality, of the land available.

I have hitherto been considering the theory of agricultural
rents; I now pass to a subject of perhaps greater present importance—ground-rents in towns. If the rise in the rent of agricultural lands has been great, the rise in that of urban properties has been still more striking. A house in Lombard Street, the
property of the Drapers' Company, was in 1668 let for £25; in
1887 the site alone was let for £2600. How do we account for
this? It is the effect of the growth of great towns and of the
improvements which enable greater wealth to be produced in
them, owing to the development of the arts, and to the extension of banking and credit. Are town rents then a cause of the
rise in prices? Certainly not. Rent may be an element in price,
but the actual amount of rent paid depends upon these two
things: the demand of the population for commodities, which

determines price, and the value of a particular site for purposes of business.

These considerations bring us to the question now sometimes raised: Is rent a thing which the State can abolish? Is it a human institution, or the result of physical causes beyond our control? If we abolish agricultural rent, the result would simply be, as Ricardo says, that the rent would go into the pockets of the farmers, and some of them would live like gentlemen. Rent itself is the result of physical causes, but it is within our power to say who shall receive the rent. This seems a fact of immense importance, but the extent of its significance depends largely on the future course of rent in England; and so we are bound to inquire whether Ricardo was right in assuming that rents must necessarily rise in a progressing state. Many think the contrary, and that we are now on the eve of a certain and permanent fall in agricultural rents; and if rents continue steadily to fall, the question will become one of increasing insignificance. As means of communication improve, we add more and more to the supply of land available for satisfying the wants of a particular place; and as the supply increases, which it is likely to do to an increasing extent, the price of land must fall. Social causes have also influenced rents in England, and social changes are probably imminent, which will at once reduce the value of land for other than agricultural purposes, and increase the amount of it devoted to agriculture. Such changes would likewise tend to diminish rent. We may say therefore that, since there are these indications of a permanent fall in rents, so great a revolution as the transference of rent from the hands of private owners to the nation would not be justified by the amount which the nation would acquire. The loss and damage of such a revolution would not be adequately repaid.

But will rent in towns fall? Here it is impossible to predict. For instance, we cannot say whether London will continue to grow as rapidly as it has done heretofore. Now it is the monetary centre of the world; owing to the greater use of telegraphy, it is possible that it may not retain this pre-eminence. The decay of the provincial towns was largely due to the growth of great estates, which enabled their proprietors to live and spend in London; but if changes come to break up these large properties, London will cease to be the centre of fashion, or at any rate to have such a large fashionable population. Politics, moreover, are certainly tending to centre less in London. And further inventions in the means of locomotion and the greater use of electricity may result in causing a greater diffusion of population.

XIII

TWO THEORIES OF ECONOMIC PROGRESS

SINCE Mill, in 1848, wrote his chapter on the future of the working classes, the question of the distribution of wealth has become of still greater importance. We cannot look round on the political phenomena of to-day without seeing that this question is at the root of them. We see the perplexity in which men stand, and the divisions springing up in our great political parties, because of the uncertainty of politicians how to grapple with it. Political power is now widely diffused; and whatever may be the evils of democracy, this good has come of it, that it has forced men to open their eyes to the misery of the masses, and to inquire more zealously as to the possibility of a better distribution of wealth. Economists have to answer the question whether it is possible for the mass of the working classes to raise themselves under the present conditions of competition and private property. Ricardo and Henry George have both answered, No; and the former has formulated a law of economic development, according to which, as we have seen, rent must rise, profits and interest fall, and wages remain stationary, or perhaps fall. Now is there any relation of cause and effect between this rise in rent and fall in wages? Ricardo thought not. According to his theory, profits and wages are fixed independently of rent; a rise in rent and a fall in wages might be due to the same cause, but the one was not the result of the other, and the rise in rent would not be at the expense of the labourers. Yet practical opinion goes in the opposite direction. From the evidence of farmers and land-agents we see that it is widely believed that the high rents exacted from farmers have been partly taken out of the pockets of the labourers. 'If there is a fall in the price of corn, agricultural wages will fall, unless there is a corresponding fall in rent,' was said before a Parliamentary Commission in 1834.[1]

Ten years ago the connection was admitted in Ireland; and the Land Act of 1870 was founded on the belief that rack-rents were not really the surplus left when capital and labour had received their fair returns, and that the only limit to the rise of rents was the bare necessities of the peasantry. In England it has been assumed that wages and profits have fixed lines of their own independent of rent, but this is not universally true; where the farmers have suffered from high rents, they in their turn have ground down the labourers. Thus even in England rent has been exacted from the labourer; and this is not an opinion but a fact, testified by the evidence of agents, clergy, and farmers themselves. What appears accurate to say about the matter is, that high rents have in some cases been one cause of low wages.

This direct effect of rent on wages under certain conditions is quite distinct from the 'brazen law of wages' which Lassalle took from Ricardo. It is impossible, according to Ricardo, for labourers to improve their position under existing industrial conditions, for if wages rise, population will advance also, and wages return to their own level; there cannot therefore be any permanent rise in them. Ricardo, indeed, did not deny that the standard of comfort varied in different countries, and in the same country at different times; but these admissions he only made parenthetically, he did not seem to think they seriously touched the question of population, and they did not affect his main conclusions. For instance, he argues that a tax on corn will fall entirely on profits, since the labourer is already receiving the lowest possible wages. This statement may be true with regard to the very lowest class of labourers, but it certainly does not apply to artisans, nor to a large proportion of English working men at the present time. With them, at any rate, it is not true that they are already receiving the lowest possible wage, nor that there is an invincible bar to their progress. Let us turn to the test of facts and see if wages have risen since 1846. Henry George says that free trade has done nothing for the labourer;[2] Mill, in 1848, predicted the same. Professor Cairnes came to a very similar conclusion; writing in 1874 he said, that 'the large addition to the wealth of the country has gone neither to profit nor to wages, nor yet to the public at large, but to swell . . . the rent-roll of the owner of the soil.'[3] Yet it is a fact that though the cost of living has undoubtedly increased, wages have risen in a higher ratio. Take the instance of a carpenter as a fair average specimen of the artisan class. The necessaries of a carpenter's family in 1839 cost 24s. 10d. per week; in 1875 they cost 29s. But meanwhile the money wages of a carpenter had risen from 24s. to 35s. Thus there had been not only a nominal but a real rise in his wages. Turning to the labourer, his cost of living was about 15s. in 1839, it was a little under 15s. in 1875. The articles he consumes have decreased in cost, while in the case of the artisan they have increased, because the labourer spends a much larger proportion of his wages on bread. The labourer's wages meanwhile have risen from 8s. to 12s. or 14s.; in 1839 he could not properly support himself on his wages alone.[4] These facts seem conclusive, but certainty is difficult from the very varying estimates of consumption and money wages. For strong proof of a rise in agricultural wages we may take a particular instance. On an estate in Forfar the yearly wages of a first ploughman were by the wages-book, in

1840	....	£28	2	0	1870	.... £42	5	0
1850	....	28	15	0	1880	 48	9	0
1860	....	39	7	0			

According to his own admission the standard of comfort of the first ploughman employed on this estate in 1810 had risen, for he complained, in a letter describing his position, of his increased expenditure, increased not because things were dearer, but because he now needed more of them.

We may take as further evidence the statistics of the savings of the working classes; it is impossible to get more than an approximate estimate of them, but they probably amount to about £130,000,000.[5] To these we may add the savings actually invested in houses. In Birmingham there are 13,000 houses owned by artisans. All this is small compared with the whole capital of the country, which, in 1875, was estimated at £8,500,-000,000 at least, with an annual increase of £235,000,000—this

latter sum far exceeding the total savings of the working classes.[6]
The comparison will make us take a sober view of their improvement; yet the facts make it clear that the working classes can
raise their position, though not in the same ratio as the middle
classes. Mr. Mulhall also estimates that there is less inequality
between the two classes now than forty years ago. He calculates
that the average wealth of a rich family has decreased from
£28,820 to £25,803, or 11 per cent.; that of a middle-class family
has decreased from £1439 to £1005, or 30 per cent.; while that
of a working-class family has *increased* from £44 to £86, or
nearly 100 per cent.[7] But without pinning our faith to any particular estimate, we can see clearly enough that the facts disprove Ricardo's proposition that no improvement is possible;
and there are not wanting some who think that the whole tendency of modern society is towards an increasing equality of condition.

Was Ricardo any more correct in saying that interest and
profits (between which he never clearly distinguished) must fall?
As a matter of fact, for the last century and a half interest in
England has been almost stationary, except during the great war.
In Walpole's time it was three per cent.; during the war it
doubled, but after the peace it dropped to four per cent., and
has remained pretty steady at that rate ever since. Ricardo
thought that the cost of the labourer's subsistence would necessarily increase, owing to the necessity of cultivating more land,
and as he would thus require a greater share of the gross
produce, less wealth would be left for the capitalist. He overlooked the fact that the rate of interest depends not merely on
the cost of labour, but on the field of employment as well. As
civilisation advances, new inventions and new enterprises create
a fresh demand for capital: some £700,000,000 have been invested in English railways alone. No doubt, if the field for
English capital were confined to England, the rate of interest
might fall; but Ricardo forgot the possibility of capital emigrating on a large scale. Thus Ricardo's teaching on this point is
deficient both in abstract theory and as tested by facts. What we
really find to have taken place is, that though rent has risen,

there is good reason to suppose that in the future it may fall; that interest has not fallen much; and that the standard of comfort and the rate of wages, both of artisans and labourers—of the former most decidedly, and to a certain extent also of the latter, has risen.

I wish next to examine Mr. George's theory of economic progress.[8] Mr. George is a disciple of Ricardo, both in his method and his conclusions; he has as great a contempt for facts and verification as Ricardo himself.[9] By this method he succeeds in formulating a law, according to which, in the progress of civilisation, interest and wages will fall together, and rents will rise. Not only is the labourer in a hopeless condition, but the capitalist is equally doomed to a stationary or declining fortune. 'Rent,' he says, 'depends upon the margin of cultivation, rising as it falls, and falling as it rises. Interest and wages depend on the margin of cultivation, falling as it falls, and rising as it rises.' [10] The returns which the capitalist obtains for his capital and the labourer for his work depend on the returns from the worst land cultivated; that is, on the quality of land accessible to capital and labour without payment of rent.

Now Mr. George's observations are derived from America, and what he has done is to generalise a theory, which is true of some parts of America, but not of old countries. His book seems conclusive enough at first sight. There is little flaw in the reasoning, if we grant the premises; but there are great flaws in the results when tested by facts. Do interest and wages always rise and fall together? As an historical fact they do not. Between 1715 and 1760, while rents (according to Professor Rogers) rose but slowly (Arthur Young denies that they rose at all), interest fell, and wages rose. Between 1790 and 1815 rent doubled, interest doubled, wages fell. Between 1846 and 1882 rents have risen, interest has been stationary, wages have risen. Thus in all these three periods the facts contradict Mr. George's theory. Rent indeed has generally risen, but neither profits nor wages have steadily fallen, nor have their variations borne any constant relation to one another. Coming to Mr. George's main position, that rent constantly tends to absorb the whole increase of na-

tional wealth, how does this look in the light of fact? Does all
the increase of wealth, for instance, in the Lancashire cotton
manufactures, go simply to raise rents? Evidently not. Wages
have risen owing to improvements in machinery; and in most
cases profits have also risen. We can prove by statistics that in
England the capitalists' wealth has increased faster than that of
the landowners'; for in the assessments to the income-tax there
has been a greater increase under Schedule D, which comprises
the profits of capitalists and the earnings of professional men,
than under Schedule A, which comprises revenues from land.
At the same time, Mr. George has made out a strong case against
private property in land in great towns; but here he has only
restated more forcibly what Adam Smith and Mill advocated,
when they recommended taxes on ground rents as the least ob-
jectionable of all taxes. Under existing conditions the working
people in great towns may be said to be taxed in the worst of
ways by the bad condition of their houses. An individual or a
corporation lets a block of buildings for a term of years; the
lessee sublets it, and the sub-lessee again for the third time. Each
class is here oppressing the one beneath it, and the lowest unit
suffers most. This is why the problem of the distribution of
wealth is sure, in the near future, to take the form of the question, how to house the labourers of our towns.

XIV   THE FUTURE OF THE WORKING CLASSES

I HAVE thus far tried to show that the material condition of the workman is capable of improvement under present social conditions. I wish now to explain the causes which have contributed to its actual improvement since 1846. The most prominent of these causes has been Free Trade. In the first place, Free Trade has enormously increased the aggregate wealth of the country, and therefore increased the demand for labour; this is an indisputable fact. Secondly, it has created greater steadiness in trade,—a point which is often overlooked in discussions of the subject. Since 1846 workmen have been more regularly employed than in the preceding half-century. Free trade in wheat has, moreover, given us a more steady price of bread, a point of paramount importance to the labouring man; and this steadiness is continually becoming greater. From 1850 to 1860 the variation between the highest and lowest prices of wheat was 36s., between 1860 and 1870 it was 24s., and in the last decade it has been only 15s. And since the sum which the workman has spent on bread has become more and more constant, the amount which he has had left to spend on manufactured produce has also varied less, and its price in consequence has been steadier. But why then, it may be asked, the late great depression of trade since 1877? I believe the answer is, because other countries, to which we sell our goods, have been suffering from bad harvests, and have had less capacity for buying. The weavers in Lancashire have had to work less time and at lower wages because far-off nations have not been able to purchase cotton goods, and the depression in one industry has spread to other branches of trade.

The greater steadiness of wages which has been caused by Free Trade is seen even in trades where there has been no great rise. But besides the amount of the workman's wages per day we must take into consideration the number of days in the year and hours in the day, during which he works. He now finds employment on many more days (before 1846 artisans often worked only one or two days in the week), but each working day has fewer hours; so that his pay is at once steadier and more easily earned. And hence even where his daily wages have remained nearly the same, with more constant employment and with bread both cheap and fixed in price, his general position has improved.

What other agencies besides Free Trade have been at work to bring about this improvement? Factory legislation has raised the condition of women and children by imposing a limit on the hours of work, and especially the sanitary environment of the labourer; the factory laws seek to regulate the whole life of the workshop. Trades-Unions, again, have done much to avert social and industrial disorder, and have taught workmen, by organisation and self-help, to rely upon themselves. Herein lies the difference between the English and the Continental workman; the former, because he has been free from voluntary associations, does not look to the State or to revolutionary measures to better his position. For proof of this, it is enough to compare the parliamentary programme of the last Trades-Unions Congress with the proceedings of the International at Geneva. English Trades-Unions resort to a constitutional agitation which involves no danger to the State; indeed, as I have said, their action averts violent industrial dislocations. And beyond this, Trades-Unions have achieved some positive successes for the cause of labour. By means of their accumulated funds workmen have been able to hold out for better prices for their labour, and the Unions have further acted as provident societies by means of which their members can lay up sums against sickness or old age. The mischief and wastefulness of strikes is generally enough insisted on, but it is not as often remembered that the largest Unions have sanctioned the fewest strikes; the Amalgamated Engineers, who have 46,000 members, and branches in Canada and India, expended only six per cent. of their income on strikes from 1867 to 1877. The leaders of such a great Union are skilful, well-informed men, who know it to be in their interest to avoid strikes.[1]

Lastly, we must not forget to mention the great Co-operative Societies, which in their modern shape date from the Rochdale Pioneers' Store, founded in 1844, under the inspiration of Robert Owen's teaching, though the details of his plan were therein abandoned. These, like Trades-Unions, have taught the power and merit of voluntary association and self-help. At present, however, they are only big shops for the sale of retail goods, through which the workman gets rid of the retail dealer, and shares himself in the profits of the business, by receiving at the end of each quarter a dividend on his purchases. Such stores, however useful in cheapening goods, and at the same time encouraging thrift, do not represent the ultimate object of co-operation. That object is to make the workman his own employer. Hitherto the movement has not been successful in establishing productive societies; the two great difficulties in the way being apparently the inability of a committee of workmen to manage a business well, and their unwillingness to pay sufficiently high wages for superintendence. The chief obstacles are thus moral, and to be found in the character of the workmen, and their want of education; but as their character and education improve, there is no reason why these difficulties should not vanish.

Such are the chief agencies to which we trace the improvement in the position of the labourer during the last forty years. At the beginning of this period Mill insisted on one thing as of paramount importance, namely restriction upon the increase of population, and without this he believed all improvement to be impossible. Yet we find that during this period the rate of increase has not slackened. It is nearly as great now as between 1831 and 1841. It was greater during the last decade than it had been since 1841. On the other hand, there has undoubtedly been an enormous emigration which has lightened the supply of labour. Three millions and a half of people have emigrated from Great Britain since 1846.

The question which now most deeply concerns us is, Will the same causes operate in the future? Will Free Trade continue to

be beneficial? Will our wealth continue to increase and our
trade to expand? On this point a decided prediction is of course
impossible. Competition in neutral markets is becoming keener
and keener, and we may be driven out of some of them, and
thus the national aggregate of wealth be lessened. But, on the
other hand, we have reason to believe that increased supplies of
corn from America and Australia will give an enormous impetus
to trade. As in the past so in the future corn is the commodity
of most importance to the labourer; and if the supply of corn
becomes more constant, trade will be steadier and wages will
probably rise. Besides, cheap corn means that all over the world
the purchasing power of consumers is increased, and this again
will stimulate trade. So that in this respect the labourers' out-
look is a hopeful one. As to emigration also, there is no reason
to suppose that there will be any check on this relief to the
labourer for the next fifty years at least. Again, there is every
prospect of co-operation and even productive co-operation making great progress in the future, though I do not think that the
latter is likely for some time to be an important factor in improving the status of the workmen. The moral obstacles to co-
operative production which I mentioned will disappear but
slowly. In certain directions, however, it is likely to develop; I
mean in the direction of manufacturing for the great Wholesale
Co-operative Societies, because here the market is secured.
Trades-Unions too are likely to expand.

Turning to the moral condition of the workpeople, we find an
improvement greater even than their material progress. When
we see or read of what goes on in the streets of our great towns,
we think badly enough of their morality; but those who have
had most experience in manufacturing districts are of opinion
that the moral advance, as manifested, for example, in temper-
ance, in orderly behaviour, in personal appearance, in dress, has
been very great. For the improvement in the inner life of workshops as early as 1834, take the evidence of Francis Place, a friend
of James Mill, before a Committee of the House of Commons
in that year. He told the Committee that, when he was a boy,
he used to hear songs, such as he could not repeat, sung in re-

spectable shops by respectable people; it was so no longer, and he was at a loss how to account for the change.[2] Similar statements are made by workmen at the present day. Conversation, they say, is bad at times, but opinion is setting more and more against immoral talk. The number of subjects which interest workpeople is much greater than before, and the discussion of the newspaper is supplanting the old foul language of the workshop. We have here an indirect effect of the extension of the suffrage. Add to this the statistics of drunkenness. In 1855 there were nearly 20,000 persons convicted for drunkenness, in 1880 there were not many more than 11,000.

Again, the relations between workmen and employers are certainly much better. The old life, as described by Owen and Cobbett, of an apprentice in the workshop, or a boarded labourer in the farmhouse, is at first sight most attractive; and the facts told to the Commission of 1806 seem to realise the ideal life of industry. The relations between masters and workmen were then extremely close, but this close relationship had its bad side. There was often great brutality and gross vice. The workman was at his employer's mercy: in Norfolk the farmer used to horsewhip his labouring men, and his wife the women.[3] There existed a state of feudal dependence, which, like all feudalism, had its dark and light sides. The close relationship was distinctly the result of the small system of industry, and hence it was shattered by the power-loom and the steam-engine. When huge factories were established there could no longer be a close tie between the master and his men; the workman hated his employer, and the employer looked on his workmen simply as hands. From 1800 to 1843 their mutual relations, as was admitted by both parties, were as bad as they could be. There could be no union, said employers, between classes whose interests were different, and farmers, contrary to ancient usage, ruthlessly turned off their men when work was slack. The 'cash nexus' had come in, to protest against which Carlyle wrote his *Past and Present;* but Carlyle was wrong in supposing that the old conditions of labour could be re-established. Feudalism, though it lingers in a few country places, has virtually disappeared alike in agriculture and in trade. The employer cannot offer and the workman cannot accept the old relations of protection and dependence: for, owing to the modern necessity of the constant movement of labour from place to place and from one employment to another, it has become impossible to form lasting relations, and the essence of the old system lay in the permanency of the workmen's engagements. Trades-Unions too have done much to sever what was left of the old ties. Workmen are now obliged, in self-defence, to act in bodies. In every workshop there are men who are attached to their masters, and who on occasion of a strike do not care to come out, but are yet compelled to do so in the common interest. Before this obligation was recognised by public opinion, the effect of Unions was, no doubt, to embitter the relations between masters and men. This was especially the case between 1840 and 1860.

Since the latter date, however, Trades-Unions have distinctly improved the relations between the two classes. Employers are beginning to recognise the necessity of them, and the advantages of being able to treat with a whole body of workmen through their most intelligent members. Boards of Conciliation, in which workmen and employers sit side by side, would be impossible without Unions to enforce obedience to their decisions. In the north of England, at the present moment, it is the non-unionists who are rejecting arbitration. And the reason why such Boards have succeeded is, because the employers have of their own accord abandoned all ideas of the feudal relation. They used to say that it would degrade them to sit at the same board with their workmen; but it is noticeable that directly the political independence of the latter was recognised, as soon as he possessed the franchise, these objections began to disappear. The new union of employers and workmen which is springing up in this way, is based on the independence of both as citizens of a free state. The employers meet their workmen also in political committees, on School Boards and similar bodies, and the two classes are learning to respect one another. Thus this new union bids fair to be stronger than the old one.

Still the question remains, Can this political independence of the workman be combined with secure material independence? Until this is done he will be always at the mercy of his employer, who may practically stultify his political power by influencing his vote, as Mr. George asserts is done in New England.[4] Among the many solutions of this problem proposed in our own country two deserve especial prominence. The first is that of the English Positivists. Comte, although he had but a glimpse of the English Trades-Unions, understood the meaning of them far better than Mill. Inspired by him, Mr. Frederic Harrison and his friends deny the possibility of solving the labour question by co-operative production or any such schemes. They rely on a gradual change in the moral nature of capitalists; not that they expect the old system of feudal protection to return, but they hope that the 'captains of industry' of the future will rise to another conception of their position, will recognise the independence of the workman, and at the same time be willing to hand over to him an increased share of their joint produce. This belief may seem ridiculous, and we must expect for a long time yet to see capitalists still striving to obtain the highest possible profits. But observe, that the passion for wealth is certainly in some senses new. It grew up very rapidly at the beginning of the present century; it was not so strong in the last century, when men were much more content to lead a quiet easy life of leisure. The change has really influenced the relations between men; but in the future it is quite possible that the scramble for wealth may grow less intense, and a change in the opposite direction take place. The Comtists are right when they say that men's moral ideas are not fixed. The attitude of public opinion towards slavery was completely changed in twenty or thirty years. Still I am obliged to believe that such a moral revolution as the Comtists hope for is not possible within a reasonable space of time.

I should have more hope of Industrial Partnership as elaborately described by Mr. Sedley Taylor.[5] This also implies a certain change in the moral nature of the employers, but one not so great as the alternative system would require. It has been adopted in over a hundred Continental workshops, though the experiment of Messrs. Briggs in England ended in failure. There is hope of its being more successful in the future, because by promoting the energy of the workmen and diminishing waste, it coincides with the interest of the employer. I think that in some industries it will extend, but that it will not be generally adopted.

There remains the ordinary Communist solution. This has taken various forms; the simplest being a voluntary association of individuals based on the principle of common property, and in which every person works for the community according to fixed rules. There are many successful instances of this, on a small scale, in the United States,[6] but we cannot suppose such a solution to be possible for society as a whole. It has only been tried with picked materials, whereas our object is rather to improve the great mass of the population. The Communism of recent European theorists, of whom the best known is Lassalle, presents a somewhat different aspect.[7] It aims at the appropriation of all instruments of production by the State, which is to take charge of the whole national industry and direct it. But the practical difficulty of such a scheme is obviously overwhelming.

The objections to a Communistic solution do not apply to Socialism in a more modified shape. Historically speaking, Socialism has already shown itself in England in the extension of State interference. It has produced the Factory Laws, and it is now beginning to advance further and interfere directly in the division of produce between the workmen and their employers. The Employers' Liability Act recognises that workmen, even when associated in Trades-Unions, cannot without other aid secure full justice, and in the name of justice it has distinctly handed over to the workmen a certain portion of the employers' wealth. The extension of regulative interference however, though it is to be expected in one or two directions, is not likely to be of much further importance. With regard to taxation, on the other hand, Socialist principles will probably attain a wide-reaching application, and here we shall see great changes.

The readjustment of taxation would enable the State to supply for the people many things which they cannot supply for themselves. Without assuming the charge of every kind of production, the State might take into its hands such businesses of vital importance as railways, or the supply of gas and water. And should not the State attempt in the future to grapple with such questions as the housing of the labourers? Municipalities might be empowered to buy ground and let it for building purposes below the full competition market value. I think that such a scheme is practicable without demoralising the people, and it would attack a problem which has hitherto baffled every form of private enterprise; for all the Societies put together, which have been formed in London with this object since 1842, have succeeded in housing only 60,000 persons. And this brings up the whole question of public expenditure for the people. A new form of association, which has become common of late years, is that of a certain number of private individuals combining to provide for some want of the public, such as Coffee Taverns, or Artisans' Dwellings, or cheap music. Such Societies are founded primarily with philanthropic objects, but they also aim at a fair interest on their capital. Might not municipalities seek in a similar way to provide for the poor? In discussing all such schemes, however, we must remember that the real problem is not how to produce some improvement in the condition of the working man—for that has to a certain extent been attained already—but how to secure his complete material independence.

Notes

1. INTRODUCTORY

[1] The sequel, as readers will observe, realises very imperfectly the plan here sketched out by Toynbee, and especially fails to deal with those portions of the scheme which are described in the words printed in italics. This is due partly to the fact that Toynbee himself found his subject, as he first conceived it, too large to be dealt with in a single course of lectures, and partly to the imperfection of even the best notes taken by his hearers, especially on the more difficult and abstruse, and in particular the purely financial and monetary, topics discussed by him.—ED.

[2] The owners of properties over 3000 acres, and yielding a rental of at least £3000 are 2512; they own in

England and Wales .	14,287,373	acres out of	34,344,226
Scotland	14,118,164	"	18,986,694
Ireland	9,120,689	"	20,316,129

—Bateman's *Great Landowners*.

[3] *Confiscation or Contract?* (Dublin, 1880), p. 23.

[4] Richey, *The Irish Land-Laws*, p. 108.

[5] Comte was one of the first to recognise this truth, and it was from him that Mill learned that 'the deductive science of society will not lay down a theorem asserting in an universal manner the effect of any cause, but will rather teach us how to frame the proper theorem for the circumstances of any given case. It will not give the laws of society in general, but the means of determining the phenomena of any given society from the particular elements or data of that society.'—*System of Logic*, bk. vi. c. 9, § 2.

[6] As, for instance, to check the exhaustion of our coal supplies.—*The Coal Question*, 247-354.

[7] Toynbee was addressing an audience principally composed of men studying for the History Schools.—ED.

2. ENGLAND IN 1760: POPULATION

[1] Mr. Thornton, member for the City of York, said: 'I did not believe that there was any set of men, or indeed any individual of the human species, so presumptuous and so abandoned as to make the proposal we have just heard . . . I hold this project to be totally subversive of the last remains of English liberty. . . . The new bill will direct the imposition of new taxes, and indeed the addition of a very few words will make it the most effective engine of rapacity and oppression which was ever used against an injured people. . . . Moreover, an annual register of our people will acquaint our enemies abroad with our weakness.'—*Vide Preface to Preliminary Census Returns*, 1881, p. 1. The Bill was carried in the Commons by large majorities, but thrown out on second reading by the Lords.

[2] *An Essay on the Population of England from the Revolution to the Present Time*, by Richard Price, D.D., F.R.S. (London, 1780).

[3] *An Examination of Dr. Price's Essay on the Population of England and*

Wales, by Rev. John Howlett (1781). See M'Culloch's *Literature of Political Economy*, p. 258.

[4] *Northern Tour*, iv. 419 (2nd edition, 1771).

[5] Porter's *Progress of the Nation*, p. 5 (2nd edition, 1847).

[6] *Ibid.*, p. 13.

[7] Slightly different calculations are made by Mr. Rickman (*Introductory Remarks to Census Returns of 1841*, pp. 36, 37), and Mr. Marshall in his *Geographical and Statistic Display* (1833), p. 22. The former gives the population in 1700 at 6,045,008, and in 1750 at 6,517,035, being an increase of nearly 8 per cent.; the latter gives 5,475,000 and 6,467,000 for the two dates, or an increase of 18.1 per cent. Gregory King, in 1696, estimates, from 'the assessments on marriages, births, and burials,' the population at 5,500,000.

[8] Mr. Rickman gives the rate of increase at 41 per cent., and Mr. Marshall at 42 per cent.

[9] iii. 57 (7th edition, 1769).

[10] 1,285,300 out of 5,108,500.

[11] 1,740,000 out of 6,017,700. These are Marshall's estimates; they differ a little from those of Mr. Finlaison.

[12] 10,438,705 out of 24,608,391.

[13] In 1700, 902,100 out of 5,101,500; in 1750, 1,261,500 out of 6,017,700; in 1881, 7,906,760 out of 24,608,391.

[14] J. Marshall: *A Geographical and Statistical Display*, etc. (1833), p. 12; printed also at the end of his *Analysis of Returns made to Parliament*, 1835.

[15] *Natural and Political Observations upon the State and Condition of England*, by Gregory King, Lancashire Herald, 1696 (printed in Chalmers's *Estimate*, 1804), p. 36.

[16] *Southern Tour*, p. 326 (2nd edition, 1769).

[17] *Travels in France* (2nd edition), i. 480. He contrasts it with France, where 'less than one-fourth of the people inhabits towns.' His estimate is, however, in all probability exaggerated.

[18] Census Returns. See Preliminary Report, p. vii.

[19] Eden's *State of the Poor*, i. 228, and Chalmers's *Estimate* (1804), p. 203.

[20] *Northern Tour*, iv. 417-19; cf. also 364.

3. ENGLAND IN 1760: AGRICULTURE

[1] P. 52 (ed. Chalmers, 1804).

[2] Edward Laurence, *Duty of a Steward to his Lord*. London, 1727.

[3] *Northern Tour*, iv. 340-41. See also *Eastern Tour*, iv. 455-56, for a somewhat different estimate.

[4] Shaw Lefevre, *Essays on English and Irish Land Question*, p. 199.

[5] Maine's *Village Communities*, p. 89.

[6] A. Young, *Southern Tour* (3rd ed., 1772), p. 384. See also *Northern Tour*, i. 160-62, where he compares the yields of open and enclosed lands at Risby and the neighbourhood as follows:—

	Open land		Enclosed
Wheat	17.18 bushels per acre		26
Barley	36	"	40
Oats	32	"	44
Bean	28	"	32

See also *View of the Agriculture of Oxfordshire*, by A. Young (1809), p. 100; Clifford's *Agricultural Lockout in 1874*, p. 121 *n.*; and Laurence's *Duty of a Steward*, p. 37-8. The latter gives the following preamble for a form of agreement for enclosure·—'Whereas it is found by long experience that common or open fields, wherever they are suffered or continued, are great hindrances to a public good, and the honest improvement which every one might make of his own by diligence and a seasonable charge; . . . and whereas all or most the inconveniences and misfortunes which usually attend the open wastes and common fields have been fatally experienced at ——, to the great discouragement of industry and good husbandry in the Freeholders; viz. that the poor take their advantage to pilfer and steal and trespass; that the corn is subject to be spoiled by cattle, that stray out of the common and highways adjacent; that the tenants, or owners, if they would secure the fruits of their labours to themselves, are obliged either to keep exact time in sowing and reaping or else to be subject to the damage and inconvenience that must attend the lazy practices of those who sow unseasonably, suffering their corn to stand to the beginning of winter, thereby hindering the whole parish from eating the herbage of the common field till the frosts have spoiled the most of it. For these reasons,' etc. etc.

[7] A. Young, *Northern Tour*, iv. 190.

[8] *View of the Agriculture of Oxfordshire*, p. 100.

[9] *View of the Agriculture of Oxfordshire*, p. 239.

[10] Nasse's *Agricultural Community of the Middle Ages*, p. 85.

[11] Cf. Tusser, William Stafford, and Holinshed, quoted by Nasse.

[12] Seven of them were for the enclosure of common fields and waste, five for waste alone.

[13] *Eastern Tour*, iii. 108-9. The italics are Arthur Young's.

[14] *Northern Tour*, i. 292.

[15] *Ib.*, 283. Other novelties introduced by him were improved drains, laying down of pastures level, instead of ridge and furrow, and improved machines and manuring. He kept upwards of 2000 acres in his own hands, on which he experimented, but found great difficulty in inducing 'the good common farmers' to imitate his husbandry.

[16] *Northern Tour*, i. 215-221.

[17] *Northern Tour*, iii. 91.

[18] 'All these doth enclosures bring,   But only a truth to express.
Experience teacheth no less;   Example, if doubt ye do make,
I speak not to boast of the thing,   By Suffolk and Essex go take.'

[19] See Houghton's *Collections in Husbandry and Trade*, quoted in *Ency. Brit.* sub 'Agriculture.'

[20] *Eastern Tour*, ii. 150.

[21] *Ibid.*, ii. 152.

[22] 'It is a custom growing pretty common,' he says, 'in several parts of the kingdom to grant no leases. Had the Norfolk landlords conducted themselves on such narrow principles, their estates, which are raised five, six, and ten fold, would yet have been sheep walks.'—*Eastern Tour*, ii. 160, 161.

[23] *Ib.*

[24] *Ib.* Caird, however, asserts that 'the present pre-eminence of the county in improved husbandry is due alone to the celebrated Coke of Norfolk, the late Earl of Leicester.'—*English Agriculture in* 1850, p. 163.

[25] *Northern Tour*, i. 282.

[26] *Southern Tour*, pp. 280, 281.

[27] Eden's *State of the Poor* (1797), i. 334. Tooke thought that Eden's estimate was rather too high.—*High and Low Prices* (1823), p. 184.

[28] *Ency. Brit.*—'Agriculture'; *Northern Tour*, ii. 127; *Eastern Tour*, i. 111.

[29] *Pamphlet by a Woollen Manufacturer of Northampton*, in Smith's *Memoirs of Wool*, ii. 320. The woollen manufacturers complained that enclosures lessened the number of sheep, but Young denies this.—*Eastern Tour*, ii. 5.

[30] An old Norfolk shepherd, who was drawn for the Militia in 1811 (when

he was probably about eighteen years old), described how the sheep lived when he was a boy:—'As for the sheep, they hadn't such food provided for them as they have now. In winter there was little to eat, except what God Almighty sent for them, and when the snow was thick on the ground, they ate the ling, or died off. Sheep were not of much account then. I have known lambs sold at 1s. 6d. apiece.'—Clifford's *Agricultural Lockout*, p. 266.

[31] 'The plough in many parts of England differs but little from the description we have of the Roman plough. Agricultural machinery has of all others received the least improvement.'—Eden, i. 442 *n*.

[32] *Northern Tour*, ii. 80-83.

[33] For Tull see *Encyclopædia Britannica*—'Agriculture,' Rev. Mr. Smith's *Word in Season*, and Day's Lecture before the Royal Agricultural Society.

[34] *Rural Economy* (1770), p. 315.

[35] *Annals of Commerce*, iii. 147. According to Defoe agriculture had much improved in the north. Davenant, in 1698, speaks of the great improvement since 1666, *Works* (Whitworth's edition, 1771), i. 359. See also Rogers, Notes to Adam Smith, ii. 81.

[36] *Duty of a Steward*, p. 2.

[37] *Travels in France*, i. 354. The average yield in England now is 28 bushels, but of course we raise part of our present crops from a non-natural soil.

4. ENGLAND IN 1760: MANUFACTURES AND TRADE

[1] Baines's *History of the Cotton Manufacture* (1835), p. 112.

[2] Macpherson's *Annals of Commerce* (1805), iii. 506. That book, together with the *Gazetteer* of the same author, has been largely drawn from in this account of the woollen industry.

[3] 9 H. III. c. 27. Coke's comment is—'True it is that broad cloths were made, though in small number, at this time and long before it.' See Smith, *Memoirs of Wool* (1747), i. 17.

[4] Defoe's *Tour* (7th edition, 1769), ii. 19.

[5] *Ibid.*, ii. 26, 37, 38.

[6] Defoe's *Tour*, i. 94.

[7] *Eastern Tour*, ii. 74, 75.

[8] Smith, *Memoirs of Wool*, ii. 542, 543, 1st edition, London, 1747. Adam Smith, *Wealth of Nations*, book iv. ch. viii. (ii. 525).

[9] *Eastern Tour*, loc. cit.

[10] Scrivenor's *History of the Iron Trade* (1841), p. 57.

[11] *Northern Tour*, iii. 9-11.

[12] Scrivenor's *History of the Iron Trade*, p. 121.

[13] Smiles's *Industrial Biography*, pp. 82, 136.

[14] Scrivenor, pp. 57, 71.

[15] Anderson, *On Commerce*, iii. 144.

[16] *Southern Tour*, p. 141 (2nd edition, 1769).

[17] Felkin's *History of the Hosiery and Lace Manufacture* (1867), p. 76.

[18] Defoe's *Tour*, ii. 397; iii. 73. The Derby mill was unique of its kind.

[19] *Northern Tour*, i. 124; iii. 135.

[20] Defoe's *Tour*, ii. 421.

[21] *British Merchant*, quoted in Smith's *Memoirs of Wool*.

[22] Anderson, iii. 252.

[23] Fox Bourne's *Romance of Trade*, p. 183.

[24] Baines's *History of the Cotton Manufacture*, p. 115.

[25] In 1719 'all the mean people, the maid servants, and indifferently poor persons, who would otherwise clothe themselves, and were usually clothed,

in thin women's stuffs made at Norwich and London, are now clothed in calico or printed linen.'—Pamphlet in Smith's *Memoirs,* ii. 195.

[26] Defoe's *Tour,* iii. 144-6.

[27] *Northern Tour,* i. 124; ii. 6, 427. See Smith's *Memoirs,* ii. 313.

[28] Felkin's *History of Hosiery,* etc., p. 83.

[29] Timmins's *Resources, Products, etc., of Birmingham* (1866), pp. 110, 111.

[30] Baines, p. 115. Ure's *Cotton Manufacture* (1836), i. 192, 193. The weaver would walk three or four miles in a morning, and call on many spinners before he could get work enough for the day.—Compare Young's *Northern Tour,* iii. 189.

[31] Baines, p. 104 *n.*

[32] Defoe's *Tour,* iii. 124-126.

[33] Near Chesterton, in Cambridgeshire.

[34] Defoe's *Tour,* i. 91-96.

[35] *Ibid.,* iii. 16, 17.

[36] Defoe's *Tour,* iii. 126.

[37] Timmins, p. 241.

[38] *Letter on a Regicide Peace,* Burke's *Works* (Bohn's edition), v. 197.

[39] *Northern Tour,* iii. 135.

[40] Defoe's *Tour,* i. 61; 40,000 were fed in Norfolk every year.

[41] *The Doctor,* c. iv.

[42] *Prose Works,* ii. 262, 263.

[43] 'Le paysan qui fait avec ses enfants tout l'ouvrage de son petit héritage, qui ne paie de fermage à personne au dessus de lui, ni de salaire à personne au dessous, qui règle sa production sur sa consommation, qui mange son propre blé, boit son propre vin, se revêt de son chanvre et de ses laines, se soucie peu de connaître les prix du marché, car il a peu à vendre et peu à acheter.'—Sismondi, *Économie Politique,* Essai iii. But see Young's *Northern Tour,* iii. 189.

[44] In 1719 it is first asserted that 'the grand cause of the weavers wanting work is the covetousness of both masters and journeymen in taking so many prentices for the sake of the money they have with them, not considering whether they shall have employment for them or not.' In 1737 we find a writer lamenting that the factors 'set up people to act as master-clothiers, on their stock, during any little glut of business,' to the great disadvantage of those who 'employ the poor in good and bad times alike.' . . . 'And hence more people are admitted into trade than the trade can possibly maintain; which opens a new door to the tumults and riots so lately felt.' —Smith's *Memoirs,* ii. 186, 313.

[45] The *British Merchant* calculated that the export trade was one-sixth of the home-trade, or £7,000,000.—Smith's *Memoirs,* ii. 112. Burke possessed a MS. of Davenant, which gave the exports in 1703 at £6,552,019.—*Works* i. 221.

[46] *Northern Tour,* iii. 194.

[47] Burke's *Works,* i. 278.

[48] The capacity of British shipping in 1762 was nearly 560,000 tons.— *Ib.,* i. 201.

5. ENGLAND IN 1760: THE DECAY OF THE YEOMANRY

[1] Macaulay, following Davenant, thinks this too high, and puts them at 160,000.—*History of England,* c. iii.

[2] *Tour,* i. pp. 159, 160. At election times 1400 or 1500 would troop into Maidstone to give their votes.

[3] Part i. book iii. p. 176, ed. 1737.

[4] *Le Capital* (French translation), p. 319.

[5] Kenny's *History of Primogeniture* (1878), p. 52.

[6] Howlett in Young's *General View of the Agriculture of Essex* (1807), i. 40; *View of the Agriculture of Oxfordshire* (1809), p. 16.

[7] 'The major part of the lands of the district are the property, and in general are in the occupation, of yeomanry; a circumstance this which it would be difficult to equal in so large a district. The township of Pickering is a singular instance. It contains about 300 freeholders, principally occupying their own small estates, many of which have fallen down by lineal descent from the original purchasers. No great man, nor scarcely an esquire, has yet been able to get a footing in the parish; or, if any one has, the custom of portioning younger sons and daughters by a division of lands has reduced to its original atoms the estates which may have been accumulated.' —Marshall's *Rural Economy of Yorkshire* (1788), i. 20.

[8] *Inquiry into the present Price of Provisions and the Size of Farms* (1773), pp. 126, 139 *et seq.*

[9] *Travels in France* (Dublin edition, 1793), i. 86, ii. 262.

[10] See extracts from Howlett, referred to above.

[11] Thrale, the brewer, father of Johnson's friend, was one of the exceptions. He was Member for Southwark and High Sheriff of Surrey in 1733. He died in 1758.—Boswell's *Life of Johnson* (7th edition), ii. 106, 107.

[12] *Ibid.*, p. 108 *n.*

[13] Defoe's *Complete Tradesman* (ed. Chambers, 1839), p. 74.

[14] Temple's *Miscellanies,* quoted in Lecky's *History of England*, i. 193, 194.

[15] Defoe's *Tradesman*, loc. cit.

[16] Laurence's *Duty of a Steward* (1727), p. 36.

[17] Marshall's *Yorkshire*, p. 54.

[18] *Spectator*, No. 122.

[19] *Travels in France* (Dublin ed. 1793), ii. 262. *Rural Economy, Essays* 3 and 4.

[20] *View of the Agriculture of Oxfordshire*, p. 269. Cf. Howlett, i. 65: 'his understanding and his conversation are not at all superior to those of the common labourers, if even equal to them.'

[21] See Wordsworth's *Guide to the Lakes*, p. 268.

[22] See Wordsworth's story of the freeholder and his tree, in Harriet Martineau's *Autobiography*, ii. 233.

[23] Baines, pp. 262, 263.

6. ENGLAND IN 1760: THE CONDITION OF THE WAGE-EARNERS

[1] Nicholls, *History of the Poor Laws* (1854), ii. 54, 55, quoting from Arthur Young.

[2] *Wealth of Nations*, book i. ch. xi. (vol. i. 211).

[3] *Wealth of Nations*, book i. ch. viii. (vol. i. 82).

[4] Harte's *Essays on Husbandry*, pp. 176, 177, quoted by A. Young, *Farmer's Letters* (3rd edition, 1771), i. 207, 208. In the north, rye and barley bread alone were still consumed. [Wheaten bread was certainly unknown among the Norfolk labourers at the beginning of this century.]

[5] *Ibid.*, pp. 200, 297. Much of the tea was very bad, and smuggled. A family at Epsom made a quarter of a pound last them for a fortnight.— Eden, iii. 710. Still the imports had increased enormously, from 141,995 lbs. in 1711, to 2,515,875 lbs. in 1759-1760.—Nicholls, ii. 59.

[6] *Travels in France* (Dublin edition, 1793), ii. 313.

[7] Chamberlayne, *State of Great Britain* (1737), p. 177. He says that 'the meanest mechanics and husbandmen want not silver spoons and some silver cups in their houses.'

[8] *Farmer's Letters*, i. 203-205; *cf.* also Howlett, quoted in Eden's *State of the Poor*, i. 384-385.

[9] Eden, i. 478.

[10] *Farmer's Letters*, i. 205.

[11] *Ibid.*, i. 301.

[12] Caird, *English Agriculture*, p. 513.

[13] Young's *Northern Tour*, i. 172; Eden, i. 329.

[14] Young's *Eastern Tour*, iv. 312-313.

[15] *Wealth of Nations*, book i. ch. x. (vol. i. 104).

[16] See Heath's *Peasant Life in the West*, p. 94, and Clifford's *Agricultural Lockout in* 1874.

[17] *Wealth of Nations*, book i. ch. viii. (vol. i. 79).

[18] Baines, p. 361.

7. THE MERCANTILE SYSTEM AND ADAM SMITH

[1] 5 Eliz., c. 4.

[2] *On Trade*, p. 131 (ed. 1692).

[3] *Wealth of Nations*, book i. ch. x. pt. ii. (vol. i. 125).

[4] The maintenance of restrictions in the chartered towns was largely due to the fact that the dissenters, who, perhaps, comprised the richest of the commercial classes, were legally altogether, and in practice to a considerable degree, excluded from office in the chartered towns.

[5] *State of the Poor*, i. 436, 437.

[6] *Wealth of Nations*, book v. ch. i. pt. iii. .sec. i. (vol. ii. 317, *et seq.*).

[7] *Wealth of Nations*, vol. ii. 326, 329.

[8] *Ibid.*, p. 331.

[9] *Wealth of Nations*, book iv. ch. ii. (vol. ii. 38); Mill's *Principles* (first edition), book v. ch. x. (vol. ii. 485).

[10] There had been earlier Navigation Acts, of more or less stringency, from the time of Henry VII. onwards.

[11] Anderson, ii. 443-4; *Wealth of Nations*, book iv. ch. vii. (vol. ii. 179); Child *On Trade*, p. 93 (ed. 1692); *Britannia Languens* (1680), 66; Richardson (1750), 52.

[12] Child, p. 98 (ed. 1692).

[13] Anderson, ii. 416.

[14] *Wealth of Nations*, loc. cit.

[15] Payne's *History of the Colonies*, 78.

[16] Mill's *Principles of Political Economy*, i. ch. 8, § 2, p. 141.

[17] *Wealth of Nations*, bk. i. ch. x.; bk. iv. ch. iii. (vol. i. 134; ii. 34, 68).

[18] In the *True Representation of the Manufacture of the Combing and Spinning of Wool* (Bib. Bodl.: n.d.), the author remarks that the importation of Indian yarn 'will hinder the consumption of great quantities of wool, by which the gentlemen's tenants, whose lands are used in the growth of wool, will be necessitated to sell their wool for a low price.'

[19] Scrivenor, pp. 73-4.

[20] Anderson, vol. ii. p. 507.

[21] *Wealth of Nations*, bk. iv. ch. vii. pt. iii. (vol. ii. p. 196).

[22] On the whole subject see H. Spencer's Essays on *Specialised Administration and the Social Organism*, and Professor Huxley's Essay on *Administrative Nihilism*.

8. THE CHIEF FEATURES OF THE REVOLUTION

[1] Vol. i. bk. ii. ch. v. p. 377.

[2] Inability to see this fact is the source of the Protectionist fallacy.

[3] 'In the cotton trade,' said Sir R. Peel in 1806, 'machinery has given birth to a new population; it has promoted the comforts of the population to such a degree that early marriages have been resorted to, and a great increase of numbers has been occasioned by it, and I may say that they have given rise to an additional race of men.'—Parl. Report, p. 440.

[4] See Jevons on *The Coal Question,* p. 109; Census Returns for 1881, pp. iii, xi.

[5] Porter's *Progress of the Nation* (2nd edition, 1847), p. 52.

[6] Porter, pp. 61, 65. Kolb's *Condition of Nations,* translated by Mrs. Brewer, p. 73.

[7] *Duty of a Steward,* pp. 3, 4.

[8] *State of the Poor,* ii. pp. 147-8. Cf. also p. 621.

[9] *Rural Rides,* ed. 1830, p. 579.

[10] Kebbel's *Agricultural Labourer,* pp. 207-8.

[11] The North and West of England in 1777; the Highland Society in 1784; the Board of Agriculture in 1793.

[12] Committee on the Corn Trade (1813). See Porter, p. 149.

[13] Baines, *passim.*

[14] In 1813 there were only 2400 in use: in 1820 there were 14,150; and in 1833, over 100,000. Baines, pp. 235-7.

[15] Radcliffe, quoted by Baines, pp. 338-9.

[16] Scrivenor, pp. 83, 87, 93.

[17] M'Culloch's *Commercial Dictionary,* pp. 233, 234.

[18] Porter, p. 293.

[19] Eden, ii. 292.

[20] Porter, pp. 151, 165.

[21] *Encyclopædia Britannica,* sub 'Agriculture.'

[22] The stock-jobbers, *e.g.* Ricardo, bought up estates, and property very much changed hands. The new landlords were probably more capable of developing the resources of their properties.

[23] Cobbett's *Rural Rides,* Reigate, October 20, 1825, p. 241 (ed. 1830). Cf Martineau's *History of England from* 1800 *to* 1815 (1878), p. 18.

[24] Report of Committee on labourers' wages (1824), p. 57.

9. THE GROWTH OF PAUPERISM

[1] *Essay on Population,* 7th edition, p. 429.

[2] Stubbs's *Constitutional History,* vol. iii. p. 600.

[3] *Ibid.,* p. 599.

[4] *Ibid.,* p. 604.

[5] Nicholls's *History of the Poor Law,* i. 36.

[6] *e.g.* Seebohm in *Fortnightly Review,* ii. 270. See Cunningham's *Growth of English Industry and Commerce,* p. 191.

[7] A law of 15 Richard ii. (c. 15) enacts that if 'a parish church is appropriated,' the 'diocesan shall ordain a convenient sum of money to be distributed yearly of the fruits and profits of the same to the poor parishioners in aid of their living and sustenance, for ever.'

[8] More's *Utopia* (Arber's Reprints), p. 41.

[9] Rogers's *History of Agriculture and Prices,* vol. iv. pp. 718-19.

[10] Stubbs, iii. p. 600.

[11] See Adam Smith's sketch of the Law of Settlement in his chapter on Wages; and on the Poor Laws generally, Fowle's *History of the Poor Law*, in the *English Citizen* Series.

[12] Laurence, pp. 3, 4.

[13] *State of the Poor*, ii. 30, 384. See also pamphlet by James Massie (1758) quoted *ibid.*, i. 329.

[14] *Ibid.*, ii. 550, 147.

[15] *Ibid.*, i. xviii. Eden himself was in favour of enclosures, thinking that the increased demand for regular labour consequent upon them would more than compensate the labourer, but wished each labourer to have 'a garden and a little croft' reserved.

[16] Howlett, quoted in Eden, i. 380 *et seq.*

[17] Howlett, *loc. cit.*

[18] 'It is not true that the rate of wages has not increased with the nominal price of provisions. I allow it has not fluctuated with that price, nor ought it; and the squires of Norfolk had dined, when they gave it as their opinion, that it might or it ought to rise with the market of provisions. The rate of wages has in truth no *direct* relation to that price. Labour is a commodity like any other, and rises or falls according to the demand. This is in the nature of things; however, the nature of things has provided for their necessities. Wages have been twice raised in my time; and they bear a full proportion or even a greater than formerly to the medium of provision during the last bad cycle of twenty years.'—*Thoughts and Details on Scarcity*, Burke's Works, vol. v. p. 85.

[19] There has always been more practical Socialism in England than elsewhere owing to our ruling landed aristocracy. The Factory Act of 1847 was carried by the Conservatives in the teeth of the Radical manufacturers.

[20] Burke's Works, vol. v. p. 84.

[21] *Farmer's Letters*, vol. i. p. 302.

[22] 'During the late dearth half of the gentlemen and clergymen in the kingdom richly deserved to have been prosecuted for sedition. After inflaming the minds of the common people against the farmers and corn-dealers by the manner in which they talked of them or preached about them, it was a feeble antidote to the poison which they had infused, coldly to observe that however the poor might be oppressed or cheated it was their duty to keep the peace.'—Malthus, *Principle of Population*, 7th ed. p. 438, note.

[23] This was the famous 'Speenhamland Act of Parliament,' so called because the Magistrates met at Speenhamland, near Newbury.

[24] Nicholls's *History of the Poor Law*, vol. ii. p. 137.

10. MALTHUS AND THE LAW OF POPULATION

[1] 'Throughout the whole of the present work I have so far differed in principle from the former as to suppose the action of another check to population, which does not come under the head of either vice or misery; and in the latter part I have endeavoured to soften some of the harsher conclusions of the first essay.'—Preface to 2nd edition, p. vii. Cf. Bagehot's *Economic Studies*, p. 137: 'In its first form the *Essay on Population* was conclusive as an argument, but it was based on untrue facts; in its second form it was based on true facts, but it was inconclusive as an argument.'

[2] *Essay on Population* (7th edition), pp. 271-80.

[3] See Nordhoff's *Communistic Societies of the United States;* and *Essay on Population*, p. 286.

[4] *Essay on Population*, 491, note.

[5] Doubleday's *True Law of Population* (1842), p. 5.

[6] *Wealth of Nations*, bk. i. ch. viii.

[7] Bagehot's *Economic Studies*, 141 *et seq*.

[8] *Science of Wealth*, 462-4.

[9] *Progress and Poverty*, book ii. ch. i. These lectures were given before the book had acquired general notoriety.—ED.

[10] Since 1860 the population of the United Kingdom has increased from 29,070,932 to 35,003,789, or 20 per cent.; while its wealth has grown in the same time from £5,200,000,000 to £8,420,000,000, or 62 per cent. See Mulhall in *Contemporary Review*, Dec. 1881. The consumption of tea per head has increased from 2.66 lbs. to 4.66 lbs., of sugar from 34.61 lbs. to 62.33, of rice from 5.94 lbs. to 14.31, and many other articles in like proportion.

[11] *Origin of Species* (Pop. Ed.), 50.

[12] 'While all through the vegetable and animal kingdoms the limit of subsistence is independent of the thing subsisted, with man the limit of subsistence is, within the final limits of earth, air, water, and sunshine, dependent upon man himself.'—*Progress and Poverty*, book ii. c. iii. p. 117. Cf. *Unto this Last* (3rd edition), p. 157-8.

[13] Eden, i. 361.—'I know several parishes, in which the greatest difficulty the poor labour under is the impossibility of procuring habitations.'

[14] *Commission on Labourers' Wages* (1824), p. 60. The number of cottages in rural districts went on decreasing as late as 1860, but the Union Chargeability Act is now said to have 'completely cured the practice of clearing away cottages.'—Evidence of Right Hon. Sclater-Booth before Agricultural Commission of 1881. Qu. 9090.

[15] Its action has not ceased, however, altogether. See Heath, *English Peasantry*, p. 36, for an instance as late as 1872.

[16] *Essay on Population*, p. 129, 7th ed.

[17] *Ibid.*, p. 315.

[18] Children were migrated wholesale into the towns from the country districts. So in Switzerland the introduction of manufactures into some of the smaller cantons, at the end of the last century, gave a great stimulus to early marriages.—*Essay on Population*, p. 174.

[19] *Ibid.*, p. 430.

[20] *Ibid.*, p. 403.

[21] Molesworth, *History of England*, vol. i. p. 319.

[22] *Essay on Population*, p. 292.

[23] *The Coal Question*, p. 170.

[24] *Essay on Population*, pp. 266, 286, 512.

[25] See M. Baudrillart's book on Normandy, where not only moral considerations but enlightened self-interest is invoked against the system.

11. THE WAGE-FUND THEORY

[1] *Fortnightly Review*, May 1869: reprinted in *Dissertations and Discussions*, vol. iv. p. 43.

[2] The employer does not say, 'I will spend so much in wages,' or 'I will employ so many labourers,' but 'I will spend so much if labour is at, say 30s., and so much if it is at 20s.' On the other hand, Mr. Heath's statement as to the farmers in 1872 shows that men may determine to spend a fixed sum; that they would not vary it, however, he attributes to the accidental cause of 'characteristic obstinacy.'—See Heath's *English Peasantry*, p. 121; *Peasant Life*, p. 348.

[3] Senior's *Journals, etc., relating to Ireland*, vol. ii. p. 15.

[4] Caird, *English Agriculture in* 1850, p. 519.

[5] Ricardo (M'Culloch's edition, 1881), pp. 54-5.

[6] See in the earlier editions the chapter on the Probable Future of the Labouring Classes in his *Political Economy,* bk. iv. c. vii.

[7] *Essay on Population,* vol. ii. pp. 64, 71, 76 (6th ed.). In reality the agricultural produce of the country was increased by one-fourth between 1803 and 1813. See Porter, p. 149.

[8] See Malthus's letter to Godwin in Kegan Paul's *Life of Godwin,* vol. i. p. 322: *Essay on Population,* vol. ii. pp. 93, 94; James Mill's *Elements of Political Economy,* ch. ii. p. 29 (1821).

[9] Mill's *Political Economy* (1st edition), vol. i. p. 475.

[10] This solution was first given by Mr. Cliffe-Leslie in an Article on 'Political Economy and Emigration' in *Fraser's Magazine,* May 1868; but its full bearing was first shown by Mr. Walker in his books on the *Wage Question.*

[11] *Trades-Union Commission* (1867), Qu. 3770 (Report II. p. 3). A. S. Hewitt, ironmaster, said, 'The rate of wages is regulated substantially in our country (U.S.) by the profits which a man can get out of the soil which has cost him little or nothing except the labour which he himself and his family have put upon it.'

[12] *E.g.,* in the horse-nail trade wages advanced 50 per cent. between 1850 and 1864, but since then 'horse-nail workmen during some time have not had half-work, their wages also declining.'—Timmins, p. 116.

[13] *Progress and Poverty,* book iii. ch. vii. p. 197.

[14] *Progress of the Nation,* 1847, p. 478.

[15] *Inquiry into the Depreciation of Agricultural Labour,* by J. Barton (1820), p. 11. At Bury, in Suffolk, a labourer in 1801 remembered when wages were 5s.; in order to buy as much in 1801 as their 5s. would have bought at the earlier date, they should have been £1, 6s. 5d.; they actually were 9s. plus 6s. from the rates, or altogether 15s.

[16] *Committee on Labourers' Wages* (1824), p. 47.

[17] *Ibid.,* p. 48.

12. RICARDO AND THE GROWTH OF RENT

[1] *Logical Method of Political Economy,* p. 42, 2nd ed., 1875.

[2] This was first pointed out in a review of Mill's *Principles* in *Fraser's Magazine* for 1848.

[3] *Works* (M'Culloch's edition, 1876), pp. 54, 55, 375.

[4] *The Present Position and Prospects of Political Economy,* p. 22.

[5] See the papers of the Land Tenure Reform Association, in *Dissertations and Discussions,* vol. iv.

[6] We find almost exactly the same theoretical conclusions drawn from Ricardo's premises by Professor Cairnes. See his *Leading Principles of Political Economy* (p. 333), published in 1864. Of course he does not also draw the same Socialistic conclusions as Mr. George.

[7] Roesler, *Grundsätze,* p. 210, quoted in Roscher's *Grundlagen,* p. 352.

[8] That is, accepting Mill's correction of Ricardo's theory.—See his *Political Economy,* vol. i. p. 493 (1st ed., 1848).

[9] *Inquiry into the Nature of the Corn Laws* (Edinburgh, 1777).

[10] *Essay on the Application of Capital to Land,* by a Fellow of University College, Oxford (1815); *Observations on the Effect of Corn Laws* (1814), by Rev. T. R. Malthus.

[11] Notice the verbal ambiguity of the text-books. When they say that 'rent is not an *element* of price,' they mean that it is not a *cause* of price. For instance, the great rent paid for mills *is* an *element* in the price of yarn.

[12] *Contemporary Review,* April 1880.

[13] *E.g.,* 'As a consequence both of their difference of situation and their fertility, in the Himalaya, the farmers low down on the sides pay 50 per cent. of the gross produce as farm rent, and higher up 20 per cent. less.' —Roscher, *Political Economy* (English translation, Chicago, 1878), ii. 19. In Buenos Ayres, 'only a short time since, an English acre, fifteen *leguas* from the capital, was worth from 3d. to 4d., and at a distance of fifty *leguas,* only 2d.'—*Ibid.,* ii. 28.

[14] Roscher, *op. cit.,* ii. 32, note.

[15] *Contemporary Review,* April 1880.

[16] Works, p. 40 (M'Culloch's ed., 1876).

13. TWO THEORIES OF ECONOMIC PROGRESS

[1] See *Agricultural Commission,* 1882, vol. iii. pp. 37-38; on the other hand, Kebbel's *Agricultural Labourer,* p. 22, and Heath's *English Peasantry,* pp. 67, 348. Mr. Kebbel's statement really bears out the assertion in the text; he says, 'The present writer could point to more than one large estate, where a very low rental has been paid for years, but where the wages of the labourer are perhaps at the lowest point, *though the attention of the tenants has been repeatedly directed to the anomaly.*'

[2] *Progress and Poverty,* book iv. c. iii. p. 229, 4th ed., 1881.

[3] *Leading Principles,* p. 333.

[4] Weekly expenses of a carpenter with wife and 3 children:

	In 1839		In 1875	
	s.	d.	s.	d.
8 quartern loaves, ...	5	8	4	4
8 lbs. meat, ...	4	4	6	0
1½ lbs. butter, ...	1	6	1	9
1 lb. cheese, ...	0	7	0	8
2 lbs. sugar, ...	1	2	0	8
¼ lb. tea, ...	1	6	0	8
1 lb. soap, ...	0	5	0	4
1 lb. candles, ...	0	6	0	6
1 lb. rice, ...	0	4	0	2
2 quarts milk, ...	0	4	0	8
Vegetables, ...	0	6	1	0
Coals and firing, ...	1	0	2	4
Rent, ...	4	0	6	6
Clothes and sundries, ...	3	0	3	6
	24	10	29	1

Weekly expenses of a farm labourer with wife and 3 children:

	In 1839		In 1875	
	s.	d.	s.	d.
9 quartern loaves, ...	6	4½	4	10½
1½ lb. meat and bacon, ...	0	9¾	1	0¾
1 lb. cheese, ...	0	7	0	8
½ lb. butter, ...	0	6	0	7
2 oz. tea, ...	0	9	0	4
1 lb. sugar, ...	0	7	0	4
½ lb. soap, ...	0	3	0	2

½ lb. candles, ...	0	3	0	3
Coals and firing, ...	1	0	1	6
Rent, ...	1	0	1	6
Clothes and sundries, ...	3	0	3	6
	15	1¼	14	9¼

[5] This sum has been carefully calculated from the statistics of Building Societies, Savings Banks, Co-operative Societies, Trades-Unions, Friendly Societies, and Industrial and Provident Societies.

[6] Giffen's *Essays on Finance*, p. 173-5. See also Mulhall, in *Contemporary Review*, December 1881.

[7] *Contemporary Review*, February 1882. He defines a rich family as one spending over £5000; a middle-class family as one spending between £5000 and £100; a working-class family, as one spending under £100.

[8] The arguments here used against Henry George are expanded in the two published lectures on *Progress and Poverty* which were delivered in January 1883.—ED.

[9] *Progress and Poverty*, book iii. ch. vi. (4th ed., p. 184).

[10] *Ibid.*, p. 197.

14. THE FUTURE OF THE WORKING CLASSES

[1] See Howell's *Conflict of Capital and Labour*.

[2] Porter, pp. 683-685.

[3] See Dr. Jessop, in the *Nineteenth Century*, May 1882.

[4] *Progress and Poverty*, book x. c. iv. p. 480.

[5] *The Participation of Labour* (London, 1881), and *Profit-sharing between Capital and Labour* (Cambridge, 1882).

[6] See Nordhoff's *Communistic Societies*.

[7] See the account of his system in M. de Laveleye's *Le Socialisme Contemporain*.